Simone de Beauvoir
on Woman

Simone de Beauvoir on Woman

Jean Leighton

Foreword by Henri Peyre

RUTHERFORD • MADISON • TEANECK
Fairleigh Dickinson University Press

LONDON: *Associated University Presses*

Associated University Presses, Inc.
Cranbury, New Jersey 08512

Associated University Presses
108 New Bond Street
London W1Y OQX, England

Library of Congress Cataloging in Publication Data

Leighton, Jean.
Simone de Beauvoir on woman.

Bibliography: p.
1. Beauvoir, Simone de, 1908–   —Criticism
and interpretation. 2. Women—Psychology.
3. Women's rights. I. Title.
PQ2603.E362Z8   848'.9'1409   74-3615
ISBN 0-8386-1504-X

Printed in the United States of America

848.914
L

Contents

Foreword by Henri Peyre 7
Acknowledgments 13
Introduction 17
1 *The Second Sex* 25
2 Françoise of *L'Invitée* 48
3 Anne of *Les Mandarins* 76
4 Woman's Curse 115
5 Girls 150
6 Simone de Beauvoir on Motherhood and "Le Dévouement" 185
7 Conclusion 208
Postscript: Simone de Beauvoir and Women's Liberation 219
Selected Bibliography 224
Index 227

Foreword

by Henri Peyre

Simone de Beauvoir has, since the end of World War II, towered above all other women writers in her own country and probably in continental Europe. The impact of her bulky volumes on *The Second Sex* has been far-reaching in America. The first tomes, at least, of her autobiography have been avidly read in translation. It is, however, not as a polemicist and not even as the urbane and candid recorder of a life, after all uneventful, that Simone de Beauvoir expected to go down to posterity; rather as a philosopher of Existentialism and as a novelist. Yet in those two fields her chances of survival must appear slim, as we are nearing the last quarter of the century. As a thinker, she has echoed Sartre's ideas too faithfully, bowed to his lead, espoused all his political views, and independently contributed all too little to the ethics and to the politics of Existentialism. As an imaginative writer, she has not once, strangely enough, presented a female character whom we might admire, or merely remember lastingly as a complex, winning, mature, true woman.

This book is easily the most searching, the most subtle, and the most courageous yet written on Simone de Beauvoir in English or in French. The author is a woman and

7

an intelligent, earnest, if judicious and dispassionate, feminist. She does not grudge recognition to the French writer as a pioneer in the vindication of the rights and the original personality of women. That movement, when we learn to look at it in retrospect and in its aftermath, may well appear as one of the momentous events in the history of the modern world in the twentieth century. Through her eagerly amassed second-hand information, through her scathing sarcasm at the pompousness of many a complacent and egotistic male writer, she has shaken many of our prejudices about the so-called second sex. Unweariedly, she repeated that one is not born a woman, even if one is born a female; one *becomes* a woman through finding oneself in a certain situation, amid a society controlled by males.

There is a lack of rigor and at times of plain common sense in Simone de Beauvoir's hasty reasoning. Contradictions abound in her passionate, polemical, often confused volume encompassing anthropology, psychology, sexology, sociology, Existentialist jargon, and literature. The philosopher's spurning of motherhood has made her own position in regard to woman's condition too exceptional to be accepted by the majority of liberated women and of feminists. Her denunciation of "the sluggish stickiness of carrion" and "the quivering gelatine which is wrought in the womb," as she designates the fetus, and her laments at woman's malediction to have to carry it for a number of months, smack a little too much, as Ms Leighton reminds us, of the Jansenist disgust with the flesh of Sartre. At bottom, Simone de Beauvoir has branded too harshly the inferiority of her sex, incapable of self-criticism and of lofty ambitions. Her admirer here regretfully has to turn into her critic. For the faithful companion and staunch supporter of Sartre, who associated almost exclusively with Sartre's circle of male friends (authors, producers, political rebels, refugees) always professed "an excessive adulation of male creative activity." At the end of her terse and lucid study, Ms Leighton cannot help feeling exacerbated: twenty centuries of misogyny are more than enough! We did not stand in need of an advocate of the second sex who is, to speak bluntly, "a misogynist." Her much-acclaimed *Second Sex* is . . . "also a diatribe against the female sex" (page 118).

One of the very original features of this fair and perspicacious volume is its close analysis of the women characters in Simone de Beauvoir's fiction. The novelist's pitfall, into which she several times regretted having slipped, was the "roman à thèse," the novel which became tempted to demonstrate a philosophical argument and which invented, or deflected, characters accordingly. None of her female characters thus abstractly and somewhat synthetically put together is, in fact, an autonomous creation. But there are at least two others, in Simone de Beauvoir's fiction, in whom we are invited to see a half-veiled portrait of their creator: Françoise in *L'Invitée (She came to stay)* and Anne in *Les Mandarins.* Each of them claims to be an independent woman through her career, through her intellectual lucidity and the nobleness of her character, through her freedom from the bourgeois conventions of married life. But each of them turns out to be emotionally highly frail, one a prey to petty and fierce jealousy culminating in murder, the other a typical romantic "amoureuse," wallowing in her love for a Chicago novelist (Nelson Algren in real life), who was soon to prove weary of her and to treat her less than gallantly in his writings. She is guilty of "spineless effacement" before the male, perhaps as a tortuous and, in effect, futile device for enslaving him. "I congratulated myself on being a nobody," confesses, somewhat abjectly, Simone de Beauvoir, or her double, in *Les Mandarins*. What is worse, aristically, both women, although copied from a real and self-probing model (or because of it), fail to impress us as convincingly alive.

Surprisingly, the novelist proved more successful in her delineation of silly, peevish, fickle, spoiled girls whose sole purpose is to enmesh men through their uncritical admiration of them (Nadine in *Les Mandarins*), through being as horrifyingly possessive of them as "a preying mantis" (Paule in the same novel and even Hélène in *Le Sang des Autres*), or acting like a sulking and obnoxious teenager with men, themselves as gullible as only intellectuals can be (Xavière in *L'Invitée*). Those female characters in Simone de Beauvoir are altogether unable, and unwilling, to view themselves critically. They will recoil before no coquettish device to ensnare a man. The young ones are insufferable minxes. The more mature ones, impersonations of the author, humble themselves abjectly before the man whom they admire. Like their creator in her fourth, and lamentably empty and tired, volume of her memoirs, they dread aging and the approach of death. They are hardly heroines for today's would-be liberated women.

Ms Leighton admires Simone de Beauvoir sincerely, as many of us do. It clearly pains her to have to concede (pp. 130, 132) the "ferocity of the female sex" of her author and "her constant bias against women." In a postcript, she voices her regret at having had to lay bare the harsh fictional treatment of women by their apologist in *The Second Sex*, and she reasserts the great debt of gratitude that all feminists, male and female, owe nevertheless to the French Existentialist muse. Her book is one of good faith, of rare wisdom, and of insight. Simone de Beauvoir herself emerges from it as an all-too-human person, torn between conflicting positions on the second sex, and courageous enough not to have bent her imaginative presentation of women in her novels to her theories or to the militant defense of a cause, however worthy.

Acknowledgments

I wish to thank the following publishers for having given me permission to quote from published works:

Gallimard, for permission to quote from the following works of Simone de Beauvoir: *L'Invitée, 1943. Le Sang des Autres,* 1946. *Tous Les Hommes Sont Mortels,* 1946. *Les Mandarins,* 1954. *Pour une morale de l'ambiguité* suivie de *Pyrrhus et Cinéas,* 1966. *Mémoires d'une Jeune Fille Rangée,* 1958. *La Force de l'Age,* 1960. *La Force des Choses,* 1963.

Harper & Row, Publishers, Inc., for permission to quote from Simone de Beauvoir, *Memoirs of a Dutiful Daughter,* 1959. *Memoirs of a Dutiful Daughter* is published in English by Harper Colophon Books, Harper & Row, Publishers.

G. P. Putnam's Sons, Coward, McCann & Geoghegan, Inc., for permission to quote from Simone de Beauvoir, *Force of Circumstance,* 1962.

Random House, Inc., Alfred A. Knopf, Inc., for permission to quote from THE SECOND SEX, by Simone de Beauvoir, translated by H. M. Parshley. Copyright 1952 by Alfred A. Knopf, Inc. Reprinted by permission of the publisher.

I would also like to thank Miss Ellen Wright, Madame de Beauvoir's agent, for her permission to use my own translations of the French editions.

Abbreviations of titles of Simone de Beauvoir's works:

TSS	*(The Second Sex)*
LFDL'A	*(La Force de l'Age)*
LFDC	*(La Force des Choses)*
MD'UJFR	*(Mémoires d'une Jeune Fille Rangée)*
LM	*(Les Mandarins)*
LSDA	*(Le Sang des Autres)*
TLHSM	*(Tous les Hommes Sont Mortels)*
P ET C	*(Pyrrhus et Cinéas)*

Introduction

Simone de Beauvoir has earned a creditable place in twentieth-century French letters both as a novelist and as an apostle and expounder of existentialism. She has also gained international renown as the fiery exponent of woman's emancipation from her servitude to her biological destiny and to male-dominated institutions. As a theorist about the "woman question" she is an acknowledged voice due to her remarkable study, *Le Deuxième Sexe (The Second Sex)*. The influence of this book continues to be felt.[1] Simone de Beauvoir recounts several times in *La Force des Choses,* the third volume of her voluminous autobiography, her permanent satisfaction from this book. She cites testimonials from numerous woman readers which amply demonstrate its profound effect on their lives and substantiate the author's thesis that it is an affliction to be born female. She writes: "How many correspondents say over and over again: "It's terrible to be a woman! No, I wasn't mistaken in writing *The Second Sex.* My idea was even better than I thought. Just a few extracts from letters I've received since the book was written would constitute a heart-rending document." (LFDC, p. 439) *The Second Sex* is not literature, strictly speaking, but it is thoroughly "engagé" and hence a work especially congenial to its author, who holds that writers should be committed and should seek to change the world.

In writing a three-volume account of her own life Si-

17

mone de Beauvoir provides an invaluable document about the intellectual and literary scene in Paris during the turbulent years before and after the war. At the same time, however, the autobiography gives Simone de Beauvoir's particular experience as a woman who dramatically throws off the yoke of a stifling bourgeois milieu to forge her own independent destiny. In a certain sense *Mémoires d'une Jeune Fille Rangée, La Force de L'Age,* and *La Force des Choses* can be read as companion pieces of *The Second Sex,* since Simone de Beauvoir several times acknowledges that her life and her ideas in *The Second Sex* are thoroughly consistent and that she has in fact lived according to her own theoretical formulations. Furthermore, in Simone de Beauvoir's novels it is the feminine characters who are the most vivid. They exemplify all the peculiar difficulties, temptations and woes that women are heir to which *The Second Sex* expounds. In short, one could conclude that the subject of woman is Simone de Beauvoir's subject par excellence and might profitably be regarded as the unifying theme of all her works.

Therefore, I propose to examine Simone de Beauvoir's novels, *The Second Sex,* and her autobiography in an effort to unravel and explore the ideas and attitudes about woman and her tragic limitations which emerge from these three apparently unrelated sources. I shall try to show what ideas are constant in these works as well as the inconsistencies and ambiguities which may be discerned through a comparison of the texts. Analysis of the novels in relation to the ideas of *The Second Sex* and to the facts of the autobiography can perhaps help to clarify what Simone de Beauvoir really feels about what it means to be a woman.

One could object to this procedure. After all, *The Second Sex* is a theoretical and polemical work, the very antithesis of imaginative creation, and it represents Simone de Beauvoir's considered intellectual position on a subject she has undertaken after enormous reading and research. Her novels have no direct relation to this work and were not at first intended as its "demonstrations." In fact, if we are to believe the author, each novel was conceived with quite different philosophical and artistic intentions. In *La Force des Choses* Simone de Beauvoir actually provides an account of the radical difference between her imaginative and theoretical writing. Taxed for her intransigeance and even virulence in philosophical controversies, she defends her polemical vigor and points out the gulf which must exist between her own fiction, which has an artistic purpose, and her abstract ideas expressed in essays where her purpose is to move, convince and, if necessary, shock. She explains how the apparent contradiction between her novels and prose essays is not a real one, and the tone of her remarks is characteristic of Simone de Beauvoir's forthright and ardent temperament:

> People tell me that in general I'm too sharp in my essays—that a more moderate tone would be more convincing. I don't believe it. If one wants to break icons, one shouldn't flatter but cause pain. An appeal to moderation doesn't interest me when I feel I have the truth on my side. In my novels, however, I stick to nuance and ambiguity. There my purpose is different. Existence, others have said it and I've said it many times, can't be reduced to ideas—it can't be stated: it can only be evoked by means of the imagination; thus one has to try to capture the spontaneous, whirling quality of existence with its contradictions. My essays reflect my practical options and my intellectual certainties; my novels reflect the astonishment that the human condition in all its aspects arouses in me. These correspond to two kinds of experiences that couldn't be expressed in the same way. Each of them has as much importance and

> authenticity for me as the other. I don't recognize myself less
> in *The Second Sex* than in *The Mandarins*. If I've expressed
> myself in two different voices, that's because this different way
> of speaking was a personal necessity. [LFDC, p. 342]

Simone de Beauvoir's distinction between a writer's "position" on something and his art is of course eminently sound. On the other hand, does this forbid the critic to compare the theory of *The Second Sex* with the treatment of women in the novels? Not at all. In fact, Simone de Beauvoir herself supplies us with sufficient justification when she says, "Each of them has as much importance and authenticity for me as the other." A study of the feminine characters of the novels measured against the theory of *The Second Sex* can be a fruitful way of exploring both the considered intellectual opinion and the more oblique and unacknowledged attitudes of the author on the subject of woman. The same holds true for the autobiography. For instance, Simone de Beauvoir presents herself as in some ways the model of her ideal woman in the autobiography, and yet all the feminine characters in the novels, even those modeled rather closely on the author, fall short of this ideal. This fact itself is revealing. Why should a liberated woman, the author of a brilliant polemical feminist document fail to create in her novels a single woman who embodies the feminist ideal of independence, freedom of spirit and strength of character?

I shall attempt to trace out the various attitudes about woman's role and character that are found in *The Second Sex* and reflected in the novels and the autobiography. The novels will be the focal point of the study since Simone de Beauvoir's literary creation is her most significant achievement. In doing this I hope to indicate how this author's life, theories, and imaginative creation interact, reinforce, and conflict with each other. What finally emerges is a perhaps less coherent and emphatically positive conception of woman—real and ideal—than is generally attributed to Simone de Beauvoir, but one which, more complex and more ambivalent, is more human even in its contradictions. The fact that a sincere and passionate feminist can herself be somewhat negative and disparaging about the female sex at this moment in history demonstrates very poignantly to me the depth of the profound prejudice against women in our culture. It underlines the need to reassess our concepts of masculine-feminine and of all our values in general so that some day perhaps the "feminine" values may find their rightful, universal place in human society, and the good qualities, masculine and feminine, will be desired and cultivated by *all* human beings, regardless of sex. A comparison of de Beauvoir's three genres can throw light on such perplexing questions as her ambivalence toward women and also call into question perhaps some of her feminist doctrines, which may themselves be ever so slightly tarnished with an excessive adulation of "masculine" values as established and revered for centuries in a male-dominated world.

NOTE

1. With the recent resurgence of feminism and Woman's Liberation movements throughout the world, Simone de Beauvoir's contribution to the feminist cause has gained universal recognition and *The Second Sex* has become one of the standard feminist classics, sold in paperback by the thousands. In a harsh and, in my opinion, unfair and male-chauvinist review of Kate Millett's brilliant polemic *Sexual Politics* (Irving Howe, "The Middle-Class Mind of Kate Millett," review of *Sexual Politics* by Kate Millett, *Harper's* [December 1970], pp. 110–29), Irving Howe taxes the author for her failure to acknowledge the extent of her debt to Simone de Beauvoir. In this one instance, Howe's strictures on Millett are just: all contemporary radical feminists are profoundly indebted to Simone de Beauvoir.

Simone de Beauvoir
on Woman

1

The Second Sex

In *La Force des Choses* Simone de Beauvoir describes the genesis of *The Second Sex*. In 1946 she had made her mark as a novelist and philosopher with *L'Invitée, Le Sang des Autres* and the essay *Pyrrhus et Cinéas.* A born writer, she felt at loose ends, eager to write but without a subject. Imperceptibly the idea for the book took shape. It started with reflections on herself and her own experience:

In fact I wanted to talk about myself. I loved Leiris' *L'Age d'Homme;* I had a predilection for self-revealing exposés where people explain themselves without pretense. I began to dream about it, and to take notes and I talked about it to Sartre. I found that one question kept recurring: what had it meant for me to be a woman? At first I thought I could dispense with it easily. I'd never had any inferiority feelings, no one had thwarted me about anything. I said to Sartre that for me, being a woman hadn't really counted for very much. But Sartre pointed out, 'All the same, you haven't been brought up the same way as a boy; you should take a closer look at it.' I did and I had a revelation: this was a masculine world, my childhood had been sustained by myths invented by men and I had not reacted to them at all the same way a boy would have. I became so interested that I abandoned the project of a personal confession to devote myself to the feminine condition in general. I read profusely at the Bibliothèque Nationale and I studied all the myths about femininity. [LFDC, p. 109]

After two years of awesome and unflagging work *Le Deuxième Sexe* was finished.

The Second Sex is a fascinating, overpowering, and finally bewildering book.[1] It represents prodigious research and enormous reading but does not pretend to be an objective and scientific study. Rather it is a strange combination of facts, history, myth, rationalistic philosophy of existentialist persuasion and sheer lyrical fllights. The book is written in several registers at once and is by turns dry and factual, lyrical, satirical, and even clinical —sometimes brilliantly lucid and acutely penetrating and again vague, turgid, and exceedingly repetitious. There is also a mixture of almost cynical worldliness and child-like naïvté, which gives it a special flavor. It is clearly, however, a polemical work, and it is an extreme book. Simone de Beauvoir everywhere insists upon the most radical extension of her theory. Her extremism is paradoxically both a defect and a positive asset since it occasionally makes the doctrine difficult to accept but it also accounts for the originality of the work. Compared to some recent radical feminist works, however, the extremism of *The Second Sex* seems mild.

In *Mémoires d'une Jeune Fille Rangée* Simone de Beauvoir describes her earliest childhood with delightful self-mockery and humor. From the very beginning she was a happy child but possessed with a marked propensity toward violence. Simone de Beauvoir does not regard this as the customary infantile resistance to adult repression but as an abiding quality of her character. *The Second Sex* reflects her own unique temperament. She relates this engaging incident:

> Protected, pampered and entertained by the newness of everything, I was a happy little girl. Nevertheless, there must have been something awry, because I had attacks of nerves and

would throw myself to the ground purple-faced and contorted with rage. When I was three and a-half we were having lunch on the sunny terrace of a big hotel at Divonne-les-Bains. I was given a red plum and tried to peel it. Mama said "No" and I fell howling to the ground. I would howl the entire length of Boulevard Raspail because Louise had dragged me from the square where I was making mud pies. As such moments, neither Mama's stormy looks nor the cross voice of Louise nor the special efforts of Papa to calm me had any effect. I would howl so loudly and so long that the people in the Luxembourg gardens would take me for a mistreated child. "Poor little thing," one lady said, offering me a sweet, whereupon I thanked her with a swift kick in the shins. . . . I've often wondered about the causes of these outbursts. I think they can partly be explained by a natural impetuous vitality and by a temperamental extremism which I have never completely renounced. [MD'UJFR, p. 15]2

Indeed it is the passion and the extremism that make *The Second Sex* significant and original. However, they also tend to provoke the reader's violent protest. In *Les Mandarins,* the heroine Anne Dubreuilh describes her first impression of her future husband Robert, brilliant novelist and philosopher, and she explains the natural effects of his dazzling intellect and equally self-confident dogmatism: "As for his courses, they were interesting of course: but after all he didn't really say anything that showed genius; and he was so sure of being right that I had an irresistible desire to contradict him." (LM, p. 44) Similarly, when reading *The Second Sex,* one wants to exclaim, "No, surely that can't be so. . . . You go too far, that can't be true," or, "But why so grim? Life surely can't be that dismal, even for a poor, downtrodden woman." Too many lugubrious case histories earnestly offered as the common condition tax one's credulity and diminish the high seriousness Simone de Beauvoir seeks to convey.

However, the main difficulty of *The Second Sex* is the

astounding inclusiveness of the book. *The Second Sex* maintains that woman should be considered a human being in the fullest sense. Simone de Beauvoir gives every side to every question, often contradicting what she has just said, answering possible objections, and then concluding with the original affirmation while not denying all the other possibilities. Of this procedure one example will suffice. Here is a paragraph about motherhood:

> Like the woman in love, the mother is delighted to feel herself necessary; her existence is justified by the wants she supplies; but what gives mother love its difficulty and its grandeur is the fact that it implies no reciprocity; the mother has to do not with a man, a hero, a demigod, but with a small, prattling soul, lost in a fragile and dependent body. The child is in possession of no values, he can bestow none, with him the woman remains alone; she expects no return for what she gives, it is for her to justify it herself. This generosity merits the laudation that men never tire of conferring upon her; but the distortion begins when the religion of Maternity proclaims that all mothers are saintly. For while maternal devotion may be perfectly genuine, this, in fact, is rarely the case. Maternity is usually a strange mixture of narcissism, altruism, idle daydreaming, sincerity, bad faith, devotion, and cynicism. From *The Second Sex* [II, p. 484], by Simone de Beauvoir, translated by H. M. Parshley. Copyright 1952 by Alfred A. Knopf, Inc. Reprinted by permission of the publisher.

Admitting the possibility of motherhood as an admirable and indeed necessary human activity, Simone de Beauvoir quickly shows that ideal motherhood is rare and proceeds to undermine the role further by introducing the "religion" of motherhood and traditional masculine sentimentality about it, thus reinforcing skepticism about motherhood's beneficent aspects. In the following paragraph she goes on to destroy motherhood altogether and winds up with a truly fearsome catalogue of sadistic and capricious mothers:

> The great danger which threatens the infant in our culture lies in the fact that the mother to whom it is confided in all its helplessness is almost always a discontented woman; sexually she is frigid or unsatisfied; socially she feels herself inferior to man; she has no independent grasp on the world or the future. She will seek to compensate for all these frustrations through her child. When it is realized how difficult woman's present situation makes her full self-realization, how many desires, rebellious feelings, just claims she nurses in secret, one is frightened at the thought that defenseless infants are abandoned to her care.[TSS, II, p. 484]

Without denying that motherhood brings out the worst in many women and that children suffer from their mothers' dissatisfactions, one must all the same take exception to the extremism of such a passage. With "almost always dissatisfied," or "it's frightening that defenseless children are entrusted to her care" we are light years away from "the difficulty and grandeur of maternal love" and "this generosity" of the preceding paragraph.

The sheer profusion and all-inclusiveness of the work are germane to Simone de Beauvoir's temperament. While a young student at the Sorbonne, she already had literary ambitions. Exceptionally intelligent and imaginative, she nourished vague but grandiose plans:

> 'It would be a work,' I decided, 'where I would tell everything, *everything.*' In my notebook I emphasize this determination to "tell all" which makes an amusing contrast with the poverty of my experience. Philosophy had strengthened my tendency to search for the essence and roots of things and their totality, and since I lived among abstractions I thought I had discovered

truth in a decisive way. From time to time I suspected that truth transcended what I knew about it: but not often. My superiority over other people came precisely from the fact that I let nothing escape me: my work would take on its value from this exceptional privilege. [MD'UJFR, p. 231]

The ambitiousness of the work, the dauntless optimism and faith in herself, the attraction to abstractions and a desire to seize the "essence" of things, and a passionate conviction about the certitude of her own truth are all attributes of *The Second Sex*.

In spite of the dizzying diversity of conflicting claims and the extremism, there is in fact a central thesis which quite clearly emerges from *The Second Sex*. The constant reappearance of certain ideas and the fervor of the diction which produces its own *parti pris* make the major theme of *The Second Sex* quite unequivocal. Volume I considers woman abstractly from three points of view: "Destiny"—her biological fate as the weaker and childbearing sex; "History"—how men have transformed her biological dependence into a condition of permanent social, political, and even existential dependence and inferiority; and "Myth"—the myths that men have woven about woman through the ages and which express their profound ambivalence toward her—mother and goddess, virgin and temptress, exalted and defamed, but always at last "the other", the inessential.[3] Much of this is standard feminist doctrine, and certainly the history of man's inhumanity to woman makes scarifying but exciting reading. No woman can read sections of this dismal record without vibrating with indignation. Also, on male psychology and the abiding sense of fatuous male superiority and importance Simone de Beauvoir is brilliantly devastating and a joy to behold.[4] Over and over again she makes analogies between man's treatment of women and the treatment of oppressed minorities like Jews and Negroes. While there is a radical difference, woman being a biologically necessary member of the entire human family, the psychological need to feel automatically superior because another group exists which is intrinsically inferior can be discerned in masculine condescension and in all the clichés about the "weaker sex." Just as the oppressing group condemns the oppressed to conditions hostile to his free development and then proclaims that all inferiority found in the slave group is "natural," so man has restricted and limited woman's education and opportunities for self-fulfillment while complacently proclaiming that she's "naturally" stupid, lazy, emotional, scatter-brained, etc. However, aside from the brilliant analysis and massive documentation of the persistence of every sort of inequality between the sexes, there emerges in addition Simone de Beauvoir's very personal and particular view which transcends the customary feminist claim for woman's political, social, and legal rights and the dignity of being considered as an equal human being with men.

In Part II of Volume I Simone de Beauvoir proposes to explain "in the light of existentialist philosophy" the development of man's oppression of woman and why man has always been regarded as superior. Not only has man decided what are the values of the tribe and imposed them upon his "inferior half", but man's original functions have been in fact intrinsically superior to woman's. This is because woman's child-bearing role only guarantees the maintenance of the species while man's superior strength and physical daring establish values. Mere reproduction may indeed be necessary, but it has no merit or value in itself. Here is Simone de Beauvoir on woman's natural functions:

The woman who gave birth, therefore, did not know the pride of creation; she felt herself the plaything of obscure forces, and the painful ordeal of childbirth seemed a useless or even troublesome accident. But in any case giving birth and suckling are not *activities,* they are natural functions; no project is involved; and that is why woman found in them no reason for a lofty affirmation of her existence—she submitted passively to her biologic fate. The domestic labors that fell to her lot because they were reconcilable with the cares of maternity imprisoned her in repetition and immanence; they were repeated from day to day in an identical form, which was perpetuated almost without change from century to century; they produced nothing new. [TSS, II, p. 57]

Man's case is radically different. Here is a rhapsody of admiration and awe. His actions transcend the mere animal condition. He invents things. He goes forth to bring home the game (in order to maintain the species it must be admitted) and all his difficulties and hardships are but a spur to his inventiveness, ingenuity and prowess. Here he is:

He did not limit himself to bringing home the fish he caught in the sea: first he had to conquer the watery realm by means of the dugout canoe fashioned from a tree-trunk; to get at the riches of the world he annexed the world itself. In this activity he put his power to the test; he set up goals and opened up roads toward them; in brief, he found self-realization as an existent. To maintain, he created; he burst out of the present, he opened up the future. [TSS, II, p. 58]

Man's power and transcendence make him fully "existent" while woman, doomed to immanence and passivity, is not really "existent" or even as fully human as the male. This argument and view of the relative merits of action versus passivity—transcendence versus immanence—is sustained all through the book as Simone de

Beauvoir's pervading value judgment. She even exalts man's most aggressive acts as part of his transcendent value. Thus back in the obscure beginnings man dimly perceives that there is a greater value in risking life than in simply maintaining the species. It is the *risk* man runs, not the blood he sheds that gives supreme value to his most murderous behavior. Here is a curious passage on man as warrior:

> The warrior put his life in jeopardy to elevate the prestige of the horde, the clan to which he belonged. And in this he proved dramatically that life is not the supreme value for man, but on the contrary that it should be made to serve ends more important than itself. The worst curse that was laid on woman was that she should be excluded from these warlike forays. For it is not in giving life but in risking life that man is raised above the animal; that is why superiority has been accorded in humanity not to the sex that brings forth but to that which kills. [TSS, II, p. 58]

The passage above would certainly provoke cries of protest from a Women's Liberationist today. I don't think Simone de Beauvoir intended any irony here because it all fits in with her existentialist categories. Her continual existentialist reduction of life itself to mere animal existence unless redeemed by heroic action (risk) makes even war glorious. One of the major feminist indictments of masculine domination has been the timeless male glorification of war and the passage above would serve as an unconscious example of what feminists mean by perverted male values. "That is why in the human race superiority has been assigned not to the sex which gives birth but to the sex which kills." That is exactly the feminist point: the male imposes his values and everyone acclaims them but sometimes they are insane.

Simone de Beauvoir's main thesis is that in spite of her biological predicament, woman need not be doomed to immanence, for it is man who has created artificial distinctions between masculine and feminine functions, and thus kept woman in a false, passive role. All the so-called feminine virtues are man-made and by admiring these, man keeps woman from seeking to cultivate the real virtues which he has reserved for himself—action, transcendence, creativity, work (masculine work which has status). Many women would find it hard to regard themselves as having less "existence" than men, but for Simone de Beauvoir woman is always "the other." In accepting the traditional masculine values as the true ones, Simone de Beauvoir paints the female condition as absolutely inferior in itself rather than relatively difficult or one which might have its own compensations and virtues.

Volume II considers woman today and the "situation" which is the key to her deliverance. The most radical part of Simone de Beauvoir's theory is her insistence that there is no innate feminine psychology properly speaking, no intrinsically "feminine" characteristics except for the physiological sexual function. All of woman's attitudes are a result of her "situation." Here is the theory:

> "One is not born, but rather becomes, a woman. No biological, psychological, or economic fate determines the figure that the human female presents in society; it is civilization as a whole that produces this creature, intermediate between the male and eunuch, which is described as feminine."(TSS, II, p. 249)

To show this process, Simone de Beauvoir describes the typical childhood of young girls, their unhappy acceptance of the subsidiary role society imposes upon them.

This is all documented lavishly with quotations from literature, and from clinical psychological cases, mostly those of Steckel. The evidence is overwhelming that the feminine condition is a trial and a lamentable burden. The weight of the negative examples and the style itself constantly reinforce this mournful impression. Speaking of the maturing girl, Simone de Beauvoir says,

> " . . . and she knows already that her sex condemns her to a mutilated and fixed existence, which she faces at this time under the form of an impure sickness and a vague guiltiness. Her inferiority was sensed at first merely as a deprivation; but the lack of a penis has now become defilement and transgression. So she goes onward toward the future, wounded, shameful, culpable." (TSS, II, p. 306)

On almost every page phrases picked at random evoke in their tonality alone the malediction of the feminine condition.[5]

The rest of Volume II is a detailed analysis of woman's traditional occupations, marriage and motherhood; woman as lover, narcissicist, prostitute, hetaera, actress, writer; woman in maturity and old age, etc. The conclusion is that marriage as a career for woman and motherhood as a justification of her existence are insufficient and in a certain sense cowardly evasions. In accepting the economic support of a man a woman remains dependent, she lives through another, for child-breeding and domestic chores are not transcendent activities or "projects" but mere continuation of life. Legal and political rights are meaningless as long as woman remains economically dependent on the male.

In her concluding chapter, "Towards Liberation," Simone de Beauvoir discusses the profound obstacles to woman's liberation since the psychological conditioning

of both sexes produces preconceptions of what constitutes "femininity". The false idea of femininity engenders a state of continual war between men and women.
The unjust imposition of immancence upon woman
makes her resentful, clinging and dominating; the dependence of woman really exacerbates the animosity between the sexes. Man's cherished domination poisons the
atmosphere and is thus a dubious triumph. Only woman's
total equality and independence can promote trust and
mutual affection. Men should welcome woman's full liberation because the old stereotypes about masculinity
and femininity are detrimental to human relations. Furthermore, the dethronement of woman from her mythical pedestal of sublime mother and fainting, delicate
creature does not mean the death of romance, love, mystery, poetry, and passion. Simone de Beauvoir ecstati-
cally envisions the glorious future where perfect equality
will not render the relations between the sexes boring
and insipid. Here is her lyrical picture of sexual passion
between equals:

> It is nonsense to assert that revelry, vice, ecstasy, passion,
> would become impossible if man and woman were equal in
> concrete matters; the contradictions that put the flesh in oppo-
> sition to the spirit, the instant to time, the swoon of immanence
> to the challenge of transcendence, the absolute of pleasure to
> the nothingness of forgetting, will never be resolved; in sexual-
> ity will always be materialized the tension, the anguish, the joy,
> the frustration, and the triumph of existence. To emancipate
> woman is to refuse to confine her to the relations she bears to
> man, not to deny them to her; let her have her independent
> existence and she will continue none the less to exist for him
> *also:* mutually recognizing each other as subject, each will yet
> remain for the other an *other.* The reciprocity of their relations
> will not do away with the miracles—desire, possession, love,
> dream, adventure—worked by the division of human beings
> into two separate categories. [TSS, II, p. 688]

Everything conspires to prevent woman's liberation. Women are insidiously persuaded to take the easy way out by becoming merely wives and mothers and conforming to the feminine myth. All of society is in collusion to make them accept their presumed inferiority and passive role. Woman becomes an accomplice in her own slavery. Simone de Beauvoir poignantly describes the painful belated recognition of women who discover too late that they have been deceived. It is the fault of everybody and no one. Men and women blame each other but both are guilty. Young women are encouraged to be frivolous about their studies and to entertain modest aims because marriage and children are always waiting in the wings. Everyone is guilty but woman is the victim.

Simone de Beauvoir's final recommendation for women is not entirely clear inasmuch as she strews the path with all the usual underbrush of qualifications and opposing arguments. She remains impressively vague about the practical aspects of her proposals.[6] At any rate, the solution is radical. All women must make themselves completely independent of men through work. The more interesting and challenging the occupation or profession the better of course. But even factory workers while they might find their children and their hearth more rewarding should "liberate" themselves and stick to their lathes. Any compromise is evasion and self-deception. To become an authentic human being woman must work in the same whole-hearted and total way that men do—for money. Then at last there will be a real symmetry between the sexes and man will no longer be able to regard woman as "the other;" the humiliating dependence upon man, psychological as well as economic, will be abolished. For perhaps the worst thing woman has had to bear is the sad fact that she needs men more than they need her. This is one of the melancholy strains of the book.

The novels of Simone de Beauvoir were not intended to illustrate the main thesis of *The Second Sex.* Nevertheless, the feminine characters do reflect inevitably Simone de Beauvoir's attitudes about women. In some ways they reinforce her thesis and in other ways they contradict it or suggest inconsistencies and ambiguities since there are certain striking discrepancies between the theory and even the "liberated" feminine characters which are difficult to explain. The significant difference between *The Second Sex* and the novels will be explored later. However, in *The Second Sex* itself there are certain paradoxes and ambiguities that emerge from the work itself, so that the positive thesis of the author seems to carry with it some inherent contradictions which are not openly acknowledged. In the first place, one is struck by the profound pessimism of *The Second Sex.* Simone de Beauvoir's view of human beings is a dark one indeed. People are frightful to one another—mothers to their children, men to women, husbands to wives and vice versa. The great majority seem bent upon domination, vengeance and a will to power, and are consumed with dissatisfaction and resentment. Loyalty and fidelity are in very short supply. The negative emotions dominate this book, and the final note, after it has been granted that some admirable women exist or that in principle generous human feelings are possible, is that such cases are rare, almost miraculous exceptions. Yet there is the contrasting current of uplift and naive optimism which rhapsodizes about unshackled human love, sexual passion and especially man's creative achievement. (Ironically, Simone de Beauvoir in this vein sometimes resembles the most uncritical apostles of individualism and good old American laissez-faire. She is very keen on "doing.") The main theme itself is the apotheosis of optimism since it really denies all cultural and biological determinism. The existentialist doctrine of absolute freedom is no doubt reflected here. If the cultural situation alone is entirely responsible for woman's immanence, dependence, and inferiority, then to change it would mean deliverance. How it is to be changed is slighted, but the Utopian hope clashes starkly with the predominating pessimistic tone.

Other paradoxes are implied in *The Second Sex.* The entire work is permeated with the sense of the glorious and unquestioned prestige of the male and the traditional masculine virtues are regarded frankly as the only true human qualities and values. Simone de Beauvoir is adamant about this. But at the same time the book is an impassioned indictment of the injustice, cruelty and egoism of the male in his historical and present treatment of half the human race. The question naturally arises: are these masculine values so splendid after all? Why should women therefore necessarily want to emulate *them?*

Likewise the entire first volume is brilliantly dedicated to unmasking the "myths" of femininity that men have created. Simone de Beauvoir fervently recommends that woman be regarded in her own humble, less exalted but more warmly human reality. But in the second volume, where she depicts the actual life and condition of women, she creates in general such an unflattering, scathing and desolate picture that one must exclaim, "But then the myths are, after all, true!" Even if Simone de Beauvoir's intentions were to defend woman's character and qualities the actual reading of *The Second Sex* seems to confirm the opposite view. That is, she castigates all the misogynist platitudes of Aristotle, St. Paul, Balzac, Michelet, Luther, et al., but she herself almost seems to illustrate their opinions. For example, she demolishes Freud's theory of woman as "mutilated man" and scorns St. Thomas' dictum of "defective man" ("l'homme manqué"), but in a way this is the essence of her own conception of woman. She even borrows Michelet's term "L'être occasionnel" (second-hand creature) and uses it without irony throughout the work. Woman is the inessential, "the other," or, as she puts it ironically, no doubt intending a jibe against Freud's theory, "the eunuch that is called feminine." Of course she always stoutly attributes all the hypochondriacal wailing, the stupidity, laziness, self-pity, narcissism, ineffectual flopping around the house, preying like vampires on men, and the general paltriness of spirit to woman's "situation." But this cannot explain the curious fact that in a book ardently *for* woman and her liberation and happiness the author does not appear to admire women very much, at least in their present "enslaved" condition. One wonders why she did not provide an equal list of splendid women taken from life, history, and literature since surely they can be found there. But apparently Simone de Beauvoir omitted the "good" woman because she does not subscribe to the traditional view of what a good woman is. The really admirable woman equal to man and as strong and powerful and free has not yet apparently made her entrance. Even though Simone de Beauvoir does admire the feminine characters of Stendhal for their qualities of character and spirit, and would no doubt concede that Anna Karenina was a heroine whom one could respect, they are all trapped in woman's timeless situation of weakness and dependency. In *The Second Sex* Simone de Beauvoir's scorn for her own sex outweighs her compassion, which she nevertheless wants to express.

The theory of *The Second Sex* can be examined from the

perspective of Simone de Beauvoir's life. What was the genesis of this radical theory and does Simone de Beauvoir's life illustrate her own precepts? This is not an irrelevant or unfair question since Simone de Beauvoir herself regards it as entirely germane. Here is a rather extended passage from *La Force de L'Age* which demonstrates Simone de Beauvoir's awareness of the pertinence of *The Second Sex* to her life. It also provides her retrospective commentary on the main ideas of *The Second Sex:*

I know that after reading this autobiography certain critics are going to be triumphant: they will say that I flagrantly contradict what I said in *The Second Sex;* they have already said it in connection with *Memoirs of a Dutiful Daughter.* This is because they have not understood my former essay and undoubtedly they talk about it without having read it. Have I ever written that women were men? Have I ever intended to mean that *I* was not a woman? On the contrary, I've made an effort to define the feminine condition in particular circumstances which are mine too. I received a girl's education, and after completing my studies my situation remained that of a woman in a society where the sexes constitute two quite distinct castes. Most of the time I have reacted to experience like the woman I was. For reasons which I exposed in detail in *The Second Sex,* women, more than men, feel the need of shelter over their heads. They haven't been provided with the temperament which makes adventurers in the sense that Freud gives to the word: they hesitate to question the basic assumptions of this world or to be responsible for it. Thus it suited me very well to live next to a man whom I considered my superior: my ambitions, although very keen, still were rather modest, and while the fate of the world interested me, it wasn't really my business. However, the critics would have to admit that I didn't attach much importance to the actual conditions of my life; I really believed that nothing hindered my desire to do what I wanted. I didn't deny my femininity, nor did I assume it; I just didn't think about it. I had the same freedom and the same responsibilities as men. I was spared dependency, the

curse most women are under. To earn one's own living is not
an end in itself; but it is only in this way that one can attain a
substantial inner freedom. I can remember now with feeling
what I felt when I arrived in Marseille—that moment standing
at the top of the big staircase—how much exhilaration I had
and the feeling of strength I drew from my profession and even
from the obstacles which it had obliged me to face. To sustain
oneself materially is to feel that one is a complete person; from
that point on I could resist moral parasitism and its dangerous
temptations. On the other hand, neither Sartre, nor any of my
male friends ever patronized me in a superior male way.
Therefore it never occurred to me that I was disadvantaged.
I know today that to describe myself I should first write, 'I am
a woman,' but my femininity has not been an embarrassment
nor an alibi for me. In any case, it is one of the *givens* of my
life, not an explanation of it. [LFDL'A, p. 421]

Simone de Beauvoir's affirmation of her independence
and her belief that her life has indeed been lived in
accordance with her theories rings absolutely true and
her autobiography supports much of what she says here.
What is interesting is her insistence in her theory that
being a woman is almost always an affliction which comes
from dependence. *She* has fortunately escaped this
"malediction" and *The Second Sex* is a sort of comradely
arm to help others to do likewise. In a footnote to this
statement she reaffirms an idea suggested throughout *The
Second Sex* that those women who refuse to accept this
version of their state are in some way guilty of bad faith.
"Whether they suffer from it, adjust to it (their fate), or
congratulate themselves for it, it is still in the last analysis
always a bad fate; since I wrote *The Second Sex* my conviction on this point has only become stronger." (LFDL'A,
p. 422) It is somewhat perplexing that Simone de Beauvoir should claim to speak for all women and to know the
sincerity of their opinions better than they do them-

selves, but mass "mauvaise foi" is not inconceivable.[7] She humbly states in *La Force de L'Age* that her own ideas and feelings are themselves rather elusive and she cannot "explain" them, although she objects to simplistic psychoanalysing which pretends to "explain" her life or ideas by reference to her past. In asserting "I did not deny my femininity, nor did I assume it: I just didn't think about it," Simone de Beauvoir is perhaps a bit disingenuous. She did after all write *The Second Sex,* which demonstrates a lively interest in the problem. The whole maddening mystery of exactly what "femininity" is is never faced up to absolutely squarely. If it is not an essence or a nature, there indubitably exists something known vaguely as "femininity," which Simone de Beauvoir herself assumes. All through *The Second Sex* we are told that it is a source of anguish for women to feel that they might not possess it, etc. Is motherhood a part of femininity? In which case, is it fair to talk about the "moral parasitism" which non-working mothers presumably demonstrate? Is economic dependence always necessarily a kind of moral bankruptcy, etc.? And in fact, is dependence itself necessarily ignoble? What is dependence anyway? Is it necessarily true that total economic independence means spiritual freedom or psychological autonomy? All of these questions suggest themselves in looking at *The Second Sex* in the light of the autobiography and they will be touched on again.

After reading *Mémoires d'une Jeune Fille Rangée* and *The Second Sex* one cannot escape the conviction that Simone de Beauvoir's extreme admiration of, and commitment to, freedom, transcendence, action, and authenticity as supreme values stem partly from the singular upbringing she received in a typically "bien pensant" French middle-class family where there reigned a curious mixture of admiration for culture and philistinism—culture being regarded as a sort of "décor" which firmly established the bourgeois as superior to less deserving classes. There was moral didacticism, puritanism, hypocrisy, and a smug acceptance and enthusiasm for the "qu'en dira-t-on": in short, the typical "bourgeois" elevation of the conventional over what is profound, important, and essentially good. Also in this period the life of a young girl *was* horrendously restricted—the sheer physical exuberance and freedom of a boy's life were denied her. Simone de Beauvoir never even learned how to swim! Girls were still commonly "married off" to suitable young men chosen by their parents and the heartlessness of this practice appalled her. Most significant of all perhaps, Simone de Beauvoir admired her own father and the men in her milieu more than the women. They seemed superior beings—better educated, more intelligent, freer and in control of their own destinies. Thus when Simone de Beauvoir describes her romantic adolescent musings about her future mate she notes:

> However, the opinion I formed of my ideal couple was indirectly influenced by the feelings I had had for my father. My education, my culture and my view of society as it was all convinced me that women belonged to an inferior caste; Zaza doubted this because she vastly preferred her mother to M. Mabille; on the contrary, my father's superior prestige in my eyes strengthened my demand that the male be superior. As a member of a privileged class and having an advantage from the start, if a man weren't worth more absolutely, I would judge him to be relatively less worthy of me; in order for me to recognize my equal in a man he would have to excel. [MD'UJFR, p. 140]

Simone de Beauvoir's acute perception of her own psychological predilections is everywhere evident; this is only one of many fascinating insights into the genesis of her own attitudes. This passage strangely reveals what is a traditionally "feminine" viewpoint, romantically insisting that a man be superior in intelligence. The exaltation or overestimation of the male probably accompanies or conceals a certain feminine self-denigration, and Simone de Beauvoir admits that her feelings stem from the superior prestige of men in her environment.

No one could say that Simone de Beauvoir is not extremely "feminine" in many of her feelings and attitudes, but these traditional attitudes are precisely what she does not particularly admire in herself or other women. A plangent protest against the feminine condition itself can be heard distinctly throughout *The Second Sex.* The "cri du coeur" about woman's "malediction" which permeates *The Second Sex* contrasts strangely with Simone de Beauvoir's tranquil insistence that *she* has escaped this scourge by surmounting the "moral parasitism" of economic dependence. If she herself has not felt this way, why is she so resolutely convinced that all other women must be so afflicted? And what has produced the strong affective coloring of *The Second Sex* where woman is alas—"vassal," "slave," "object," "prey," "victim," "passivity," "dependent," "immanence," "parasite," "prisoner"—where she is ineluctably "the other"? Perhaps in the course of this study some of this ambiguity can be more fully unraveled and explored if not explained.

NOTES

1. Elizabeth Hardwick calls it aptly "a madly sensible and confused tome" in Elizabeth Hardwick, "The Subjection of Women," review of *The Second Sex,* by Simone de Beauvoir, *Partisan Review* 20, no. 3 (May–June 1953): 321–31.

2. Simone de Beauvoir returns often to her extremism, or her "goût

d'absolu" in the autobiography. In *Mémoires d'une Jeune Fille Rangée* it is linked to a certain seriousness and solemnity of her character as an adolescent, bound up with a romantic, absolutist temperament. She writes: "Analysing my character in the middle of autumn, what I noticed first of all was what I call my serious side: an austere and implacable seriousness whose cause I don't understand but which I submit to as a kind of necessary exigency in my character. Since my childhood I've always been obstinate and given to extremes, and I've always been proud of it. Others might be half-hearted in their faith or skepticism or in their desires or plans; I scorned their tepidity. I would always be passionate in my emotions, ideas and enterprises; I took nothing lightly and as in my early childhood I wanted my whole life to be justified by a kind of necessity. This stubbornness I realized deprived me of some good traits but there was no question of separating it from myself. My serious side, that *was* me, and I valued the real me very highly." (MD'UJFR, p. 207)

3. Elizabeth Hardwick, 321, wittily evokes Simone de Beauvoir's view of the unrewarding fate of the second sex—woman, "Sisyphean goddess of the dust-pile!"

4. Claude Mauriac had the bad luck to write the following paragraph about woman writers: *"We* listen with an air of polite indifference . . . the most brilliant among them knowing well that her wit and intelligence reflects in a rather striking manner ideas which came from *us."* Simone de Beauvoir seizes this absurdly fatuous "we" and makes short work of Claude Mauriac: "What's remarkable is that with the equivocal use of *us* he identifies *himself* with Saint Paul, Hegel, Lenin, Nietszche and from the height of their grandeur he looks down in disdain on the little band of women who have the temerity to speak to him on a level of equality; to tell the truth, I know more than one woman who wouldn't have the patience to treat Mauriac with 'an air of polite indifference.' " (LDS, I, p. 26)

5. Some examples picked at random: "Her whole body is experienced with uneasiness." " . . . her strange and bothersome breasts are a burden," . . . "Her whole body is a source of embarrassment." . . . " 'boys are better.' This is a debilitating conviction." . . . "Any self-assertion will diminish her femininity and her attractiveness." (TSS, II, pp. 308, 310, 313, 314, 316)

6. Simone de Beauvoir is an impassioned rationalist and cannot be too concerned with squalid, empirical objections. In the last chapter, one is surprised to find: "As a matter of fact, man, like woman, is flesh, therefore passive, the plaything of his hormones and of the species, the restless prey of his desires." (TSS, II, p. 685) This is indeed reassuring to a poor, passive feminine creature, but this admission has little effect after two volumes documenting woman's passivity, animality and subservience to hormones.

7. As Elizabeth Hardwick says, "These creatures' claims are admitted quite fully throughout the book, but always with the suggestion that those women who seem to be 'existents' really aren't and those who insist they find fulfillment in the inferior role are guilty of 'bad faith!' " Hardwick, p. 324.

2

Françoise of *L'Invitée*

AUTONOMY VS. DEPENDENCY, REASON VS. EMOTION: THE "SITUATION" AS KEY TO CHARACTER

L'Invitée is perhaps Simone de Beauvoir's most powerful novel. It is the result of a patient apprenticeship in writing novels which pleased neither Simone de Beauvoir nor her publisher. The impetus for the design of *L'Invitée* came from Sartre, who urged her to have the boldness to model her heroine on herself. She relates in her autobiography how Sartre's suggestion both stimulated and terrified her:

> 'After all, why not put yourself in what you write?' he said to me with sudden vehemence. 'You're more interesting than all these Lisas and Renées.' His remark made me flush, it was hot and the room was oppressively smoky and loud with people's talk around us, and I felt as though I had received a blow on the head. 'I'd never dare do that,' I said, 'to reveal myself, exposed and vulnerable, in a book, not to maintain a certain distance and to compromise myself—no, the idea frightens me.' 'Dare to do it,' said Sartre. [LFDL'A, p. 363]

Simone de Beauvoir's first abortive attempt to follow this advice was turned down by the publisher who said it had some merit as "a description of manners" but lacked

48

originality. This verdict surprised Simone de Beauvoir inasmuch as she had thought she was creating, not a "description of manners" but rather "subtle psychological observations." With great good humor and reflecting wisely on the vast abyss between intention and realization in artistic creation, she shelved *La Primauté du Spirituel,* which contained bare sketches of some of the characters who reappear in *L'Invitée* but which was more conventional and diffuse. Simone de Beauvoir did draw on her own life in this first attempt but not in the starkly effective way that she finally succeeded in doing in *L'Invitée.* She says: "I didn't have the nerve (at that time) to get to the heart of the matter and openly call into question the woman of thirty that I was." (LFDL'A, p. 365)

In *L'Invitée* the heroine Françoise's point of view dominates the work, and since she is a fictional projection of the author's self, she does indeed "call into question the thirty-year-old woman that I was." The emotional intensity of *L'Invitée* comes not only from the mastery of form and style but from the sincerity of the author's own feelings, which are perilously involved in a book seeking to "call into question" her own life. Sincerity and experience are certainly not guarantees of artistic excellence, but in this novel Simone de Beauvoir seems to have found the formula for transforming autobiographical material into a novel which brilliantly achieves her earlier aim of creating "subtle psychological effects."

Of course the relation of autobiography to fiction is hideously complex, and one might also attribute the defects of *L'Invitée* to the author's personal involvement. In *La Force de L'Age* Simone de Beauvoir dissects her novel with the acumen of an impartial critic and agrees that the murder of Xavière by Françoise is a flaw. She says: "Without doubt, the ending which I have often been

reproached with is the weakest part of the book. . . .
Novelists often forget that in real life there is an enormous difference between dreaming of murder and the
act of murder; killing is not a daily occurrence. The
Françoise that I created is as incapable of it as I am."
(LFDL'A, p. 391) Nonetheless, Simone de Beauvoir
goes on to justify this conclusion in terms of her own
emotional therapy. Even if it is artistically unsatisfactory,
the ending came from a profound need of the author to
exorcize her own demons. She explains:

> At first by killing Olga [real-life model of Xavière] on paper
> I got rid of the irritation and malice I had felt on her account;
> our friendship was improved by my being able to exorcize the
> bad memories which had got mixed with the good; above all,
> by liberating Françoise, through a crime, from the dependency
> that her love for Pierre encouraged, I found my own au-
> tonomy. Re-reading these final pages, today inert and frozen,
> I find it difficult to believe that while revising them I actually
> felt a lump in my throat as though I had the weight of a real
> crime upon my shoulders. Nevertheless, that's the way it was.
> Pen in hand, I felt positively terrified by the experience of
> separation. The murder of Xavière may seem like a hasty and
> clumsy resolution of a drama that I didn't know how to end.
> But, on the contrary, it was the motive and the 'raison d'être'
> of the entire novel. [LFDL'A, pp. 391–92]

Simone de Beauvoir does not apparently experience
the act of writing as arising from "emotion recollected in
tranquillity." Her burning account of the intimate connection between life and fiction is a fine example of the
emotional catharis and subsidiary pleasures to be derived
from writing novels. *L'Invitée* does have a close equivocal
relation to its author's experience which in part accounts
for its special emotional pitch of intensity. Simone de
Beauvoir has managed to distill the disturbing and dis-

orderly emotions of life into a disturbing but well-ordered novel.

L'Invitée may be characterized as a philosophical novel in the sense that it does demonstrate a particular thesis of the author, indicated by the epigraph from Hegel: "every mind seeks the death of every other mind." Simone de Beauvoir stoutly maintains that *L'Invitée* is not a "roman à thèse," but in the same paragraph she describes her heroine's actions, which certainly have an existentialist air about them: "Françoise gave up trying to find a solution to the problem of co-existence; she submitted to the other as a scandalous and inevitable condition; she resisted this impossible condition by committing an act which was equally brutal and irrational—murder." (LFDL'A, p. 391) Merleau-Ponty[1] finds the chief merit of the novel in its metaphysical implications and Hazel Barnes[2] did an interesting analysis of *L'Invitée* as a step-by-step novelistic reenactment of Sartre's *L'Etre et Le Néant.* Yet the force and subtle psychological delicacy of the novel come not from the metaphysical abstractions which sometimes intrude dangerously, but from the web of inchoate feelings and the undercurrents of sympathy, hostility, and misunderstanding which envelop the characters. They often act with what they regard as perfect lucidity and good will, but they inflict, unwillingly it would seem, intolerable pain upon each other. Georges Blin singles out a notable passage of *L'Invitée* for comment:

> Torn between a story to tell and the need to demonstrate a thesis, Simone de Beauvoir sometimes seems to question her procedure along the way. At least she doesn't ignore the difficulties of the genre she has chosen; she points them out and she justifies herself in a dialogue which is both unobtrusive and

artful: 'What surprises me,' Pierre said to Françoise, 'is that you
are affected in such a concrete way by a metaphysical situation.'
'But a metaphysical situation *is* concrete,' Françoise protested,
'for me an idea either is experienced, or it's only theoretical,
it doesn't count.' That is how the heroine in the midst of the
novel anticipates and forestalls the objections she knows will
be made to the author.[3]

This remark of Françoise is both psychologically and
philosophically fitting since she is a passionate but rationalistic person who takes her ideas extremely seriously.
And existentialism always insists that mere academic
philosophy is not worthy of the name. But the point is
that Françoise often talks like a professor of philosophy
and employs improbable existentialist jargon. This is certainly not what is meant by "living one's philosophy."[4]
Blin describes the peculiar quality of the novel which
does not reside in its metaphysics:

> Perhaps the opacity of this story arises elsewhere, not from
> technical blunders, but from the instability of the characters
> themselves—the ones who gratuitously suffer from tempera-
> mental excesses, who lack deep convictions, are not strongly
> motivated and who, in a pinch, act against their own best
> interests. They provide, in the absence of clear-cut outlines,
> that kind of density and disquiet which we recognize, with
> pleasure, as characteristic features of the Russian novel.[5]

Simone de Beauvoir in her exegesis of *L'Invitée* concurs
in this estimate of her work. Here she describes the
technique of her novel and her attempt to create an
atmosphere of human non-rapport and misunderstanding:

> As for the aesthetic of *L'Invitée;* I have explained the precepts
> which it rests on; I'm delighted to have followed these; my

book owes whatever excellence it has to them. Thanks to the ignorance in which I keep my heroes, the episodes are often as enigmatic as in a good novel by Agatha Christie; the reader does not immediately notice the import of the episode; gradually new developments and discussions uncover some unsuspected aspects; Pierre can endlessly analyse some gesture of Xaviere's which Françoise had barely noticed and whose meaning can never be completely deciphered because no one has a final edge on the truth. The most successful passages of the novel convey ambiguous meanings which are like those encountered in real life. [LFDL'A, p. 396]

The central character of *L'Invitée,* Françoise Miguel, will be the main focus of my attention. Françoise corresponds in many ways to the ideal "emancipated" woman of *The Second Sex.* Frankly modeled on Simone de Beauvoir at thirty, she appears at first glance to have surmounted the vicissitudes of youth and have "found herself." She is a liberated woman: she writes novels and collaborates in the theater with her companion and lover, Pierre Labrousse, actor and director. She lives an independent life in Paris; she has renounced marriage, children, and narrow bourgeois family ties. She has therefore "realized" herself through her work while having found happiness and companionship in love. This apparent success is only a mirage, however, and although her friends regard Françoise as a tower of strength and an enviably self-assured and authentic person, the novel gradually reveals her inner weakness and dependency. This weakness, exacerbated by her relations with the other characters, each implacably mysterious in his own impenetrability, finally sweeps her along to the irremediable and somber conclusion.

Françoise is a thoroughly sympathetic heroine and the novel is told from the perspective of her consciousness so that the reader identifies mainly with her sufferings and dilemmas. He realizes soon that Françoise actually is not in full control of her destiny despite her independent job and enlightened thinking. Indeed, like all of Simone de Beauvoir's heroines, she is "une grande amoureuse," a cateory not regarded by the author as leading to authentic existence. To live for love, even the most exalted, entails a kind of slavery and self-debasement because of the ultimate dependency entailed. It is interesting to observe, in fact, how ridiculously unimportant Francoise's work seems to her, how it recedes into the background as the novel progresses and scarcely leaves a trace. In Chapter I Françoise is presumably writing a novel: "The typewriter was clicking away. . . . She finishes her work, thinking of Pierre on the train returning to Paris, imagining their meeting. 'Finished,' Françoise said, 'As long as he likes it!' I think he'll like it.' " (*L'Invitée,* p. 15) This is one of the rare references to her work, and it is primarily Pierre's approval which concerns her. In *The Second Sex,* Simone de Beauvoir is adamant in her denouncement of woman's living "through" a man, but Françoise, modeled on herself at thirty, is in her own way as emotionally dependent on a man as the most conventional wife or mistress.[6] Pierre's career interests Françoise much more than her own, and she suffers when he treats *his* work frivolously or neglects it. Viewed from this angle, the whole novel is, then, a gradual unveiling of Francoise's tragic dependency which she has up until now concealed from herself. It stems not so much from her love for Pierre, but from a more fundamental failure to achieve sufficient force in her own character. *The Second Sex* holds that woman can achieve "substantial inner freedom" through an absorbing and satisfying career just as a man does, but Françoise demonstrates quite poignantly that this is not so easily attained. The power of emotional ties are such that authentic work as an ideal bulwark against emotional disaster is tragically insufficient. *L'Invitée* also suggests that character is profoundly rooted in individual psychology and that the "situation" of woman cannot alone be responsible for behavior. While *The Second Sex* serenely and dogmatically pronounces that woman should not succumb to "moral parasitism" and should refuse to live "through" a man, Françoise's struggle points up the weakness of such abstract formulas. Her inner conflicts, her simultaneous lucidity and self-deception, her horror of dependency, yet her incapacity to recognize her total surrender to the ideas and imperatives of another, paint a truer picture, and, by the same token, provide the overwhelming dramatic impact of the book. For this is a novel about jealousy among high-minded people who believe that jealousy is an unworthy, paltry and base emotion, and about dependency and weakness in a heroine who regards freedom, independence, and courage as the supreme human qualities. The discord between ideas and feelings, thought and deeds, intentions and results, lofty aims and less than lofty behavior, and egoism disguised as generosity accounts for the striking emotive force of the novel which weaves a kind of Dostoyevskyan imbroglio of ambiguous human strivings, self-deception and cross purposes.

Since the distress of Françoise reflects certain real experiences of Simone de Beauvoir, it is instructive to turn to the autobiography and examine the audacious experiment and quite gloriously unique romance of Simone de Beauvoir and Jean-Paul Sartre. The fundamental conflict in the novel appears indeed to spring from their rather remarkable attempt to live by the light of pure reason and good will. In reading the autobiography one feels that Jean-Paul Sartre was a miraculous answer to Simone de Beauvoir's imperious psychological needs; one could say ironically, although with perfect justice, that the "marriage" of these two incredibly gifted, strong-willed, romantic rationalists was indeed "made in heaven." Simone de Beauvoir's account of the "coup de foudre" in *Mémoires d'une Jeune Fille Rangée* leaves no doubt about the rare good chance of their encounter. From the first moment Sartre overwhelmed her by his dazzling intelligence, their unique affinities were immediately recognized and their common fate was sealed in an almost traditional manner. This was a "marriage of true minds." Simone de Beauvoir recounts: "It was the first time in my life that I felt dominated by someone else intellectually. . . . Sartre lived up exactly to the man I had dreamed of at fifteen; he was my double in whom I re-discovered all my own tastes and enthusiasms, refined to the point of incandescence; with him I could always share everything. When I left him at the end of August, I knew he would never again leave my life." (MD'UJFR, p. 331) In spite of the lofty disdain of conventional morality which united these two passionate iconoclasts, one can detect on Simone de Beauvoir's part some of the more traditional "weaker sex" attitudes toward love. The desire to be dominated, to agree on every single thing and to always be able to "look up to" the man seems "feminine" in the old-fashioned way, perhaps a bit masochistic in the way women are supposed to be.[7] The mutual respect and admiration shines out radiantly from the autobiography, but nonetheless it is striking how Sartre dominates the couple, not only by his intellectual virtuosity, but also emotionally. According to her own account, through the years Simone de Beauvoir valiantly battled with Sartre on every conceivable issue, but she always at last ended

up in his camp. When the celebrated pact is made between them about "necessary" and "contingent" love,
one can't help remarking that it is Sartre's idea. The
young Simone de Beauvoir, enrapt, and of course shar-
ing most of his predilections, finds the proposal eminently reasonable and feasible, but most of the charm of
it seems to have come from the hypnotic spell that this
prestidigitator of reason exercized over her.

Both of them were fanatically devoted to freedom and
had a boundless faith in the power of reason and will to
conquer the "monsters" of the affective life. Simone de
Beauvoir describes their attitude: "We remained set in
our rationalist and voluntarist attitude; we thought that
if a person were really lucid and clear, freedom might
triumph over traumas, complexes, memories and influences." (LFDL'A, p. 25) It appears, however, that Sartre
was even more attracted to freedom than Simone de
Beauvoir: "Sartre didn't feel designed for monogamy; he
delighted in the company of women whom he found less
ludicrous than men; he didn't intend to renounce
forever, at the age of twenty-three, their fascinating
diversity. Between *us,* he explained to me, using a
vocabulary dear to him, it was a question of "necessary"
love; it was also right and proper that we experience
"contingent" loves." (LFDL'A, p. 26) Then Simone de
Beauvoir continues in a tone remarkable for its bizarre
lyricism and belief in eternal love which will be spiced by
the charm of side adventures: "We belonged to the same
race and our understanding would last as long as we
would: it couldn't make up for the ephemeral delight of
our encounters with different beings; how could we be
content, deliberately, to not experience the gamut of
astonishment, regret, nostalgia and pleasure which we
were also capable of experiencing. We pondered this

question long and deeply." (LFDL'A, p. 26) This is an astonishing recital with its rather touching faith in the possibility of regulating one's love life *reasonably* so that *all* of its delights can be cozily enjoyed. The quality of the attachment is unmistakable, but it must be said that passion does not seem to have carried the day when both lovers, at the very beginning of an eternal union, solemnly plan to be unfaithful. At any rate, Simone de Beauvoir and Sartre decide to live together for two years, then separate temporarily but separation will not alter their eternal union of minds. Here is de Beauvoir's account of the agreement: "Never would we become alien to each other, never would one of us have to appeal to the other in vain, and nothing could prevail against this alliance; but it did not have to degenerate into constraint and habit: we would preserve the relationship from this sort of paltriness at all cost. I acquiesced." (LFDL'A, p. 27) She "acquiesces" in Sartre's plan, and perhaps the choice of verb is significant, implying some preliminary resistance.

I dwell on this singular arrangement and the perhaps somewhat docile acceptance of Sartre's scheme by the admiring and committed young girl in love, because this kind of enlightened and "rational" relationship is at the center of *L'Invitée.* The belief that utter honesty, fairness, reason, good will and generosity can chart the course of any intricate human relationship is the cornerstone of Françoise's and Pierre's philosophy. Furthermore, in spite of their apparent unanimity in these matters, it becomes evident that Françoise defers to Pierre and accepts all of these cheerful rationalistic axioms without question and without even conceiving of or daring to oppose them, much in the same way that Simone de Beauvoir did. It is against this background of enlight-

ened good sense and scorn for demeaning emotions such
as jealousy that the drama of Françoise takes place. For
she is caught in the unenviable trap of gradually realizing
that she cannot admit what she feels, of losing her good
opinion of herself because she falls prey to the very jealousy which she has deemed unworthy. She must appear
to live by the abstract principles of Pierre, which are
quite inadequate to sustain her.

The experiment which is at the core of this diabolical
trap in *L'Invitée* is the attempt to form a sort of trio
between Francoise, Pierre, and Xavière. They will com-
prise a superior relationship unfettered by the sordid
concerns of jealousy and possessiveness, so that the re-
sulting harmony will be richer and more humanly interesting than the accord of a well-attuned couple. Xavière
is a young, charming, capricious, and self-willed girl who
admires Françoise extravagantly and is desolate at the
prospect of wasting her youth in the arid desert of
Rouen. Françoise and Pierre decide to rescue her. They
help her to stay in Paris, but gradually their fascination
with her becomes almost a pathological obsession. They
conceive of the trio as a sort of experiment in living
which will be a triumph of enlightened human conduct.
While they talk benignly about the charms of the trio,
their emotions become more and more ambivalent, obscure, and downright hostile. It is clear to the reader,
though not to them, that this experiment is gradually
eroding the relationship of Françoise and Pierre and
progressively inflicting subtle tortures on all three. Françoise's suffering attains the greatest paroxysm since it is
Françoise with whom the reader identifies.

In short, the trio becomes inadvertently a complicated
example of "bad faith." The constant and relentless ratiocination and the remorseless psychological analyses of

Françoise and Pierre are just a sort of smoke screen for their real emotions which they feel half-heartedly, distort, deny, or suppress. The split between thought and feeling is quite pronounced. There is profound irony in the situation, because Pierre and Françoise detest above all inauthenticity and falseness and have such high standards about honor and truthfulness that the other characters look up to them as models of excellence. Yet, in spite of their superior qualities and noble intentions, the trio becomes an inferno of mutually inflicted cruelty, self-deception, and even ignoble behavior.

The beginning of the novel underlines the singular attachment and understanding between Pierre and Françoise. Pierre has had amorous escapades, but they have meant less than nothing to him and therefore have in no way altered their basically profound and admirable relationship. Similarly, when Simone de Beauvoir recounts the first of Sartre's "contingent" loves in the autobiography she says she was not jealous because she had been warned beforehand: "It was nevertheless the first time since we knew each other that another woman counted for Sartre, and jealousy is not a feeling that I underestimate nor of which I am incapable. But this flirtation of his didn't hit me unexpectedly and it didn't change at all my opinion of our own life together, since Sartre had warned me from the beginning that he would have adventures. I had accepted the principle and I accepted the fact without too much difficulty." (LFDL'A, p. 211) Françoise does not apparently altogether share Pierre's (or Simone de Beauvoir's) insouciance about this matter, although she will not admit to being jealous. But she tells Pierre she cannot help it, but she is only interested in total commitment to one person. Here is their dialogue:

'These little flirtations don't amuse me much any more,' Pierre
said. 'If I were at least a terribly sensual kind of man, but I
don't even have that excuse.' He looked at Françoise, per-
plexed. 'All there is to it is that I like beginnings. Don't you
understand that?'
'Perhaps,' said Françoise, 'But for me, no. I'm not interested
in an adventure with no future.'
'No?' said Pierre.
'No,' she said, 'I can't help it: I'm a faithful woman.'
'You can't talk about fidelity or infidelity between us,' said
Pierre, and he drew her close. 'You and I, we are only one
person. It's true, you know, you couldn't define one of us
without the other.' [*L'Invitée*, p. 26]

Already here one senses a discrepancy between what
Françoise thinks and feels, a state of mind which may be
unconsciously Simone de Beauvoir's own. The way she
amiably subscribes to Pierre's somewhat sophistical arguments is characteristic of her behavior. She uses the word
"faithful" in the customary sense, while he blithely ann-
hilates this meaning in a sort of élan about their superior
relationship which is no doubt sincere and which disarms
Françoise. Faithfulness is somehow made to appear
rather petty and irrelevant to their grander view of things
and one feels that Françoise won't venture in this direc-
tion again. There follows an interior dialogue in which
she thinks about the place Pierre holds in her life, and
how they can tell each other *everything* with implacable
honestly:

Until she had told Pierre all about it, nothing in her life was
completely real. Before when Pierre used to intimidate her
there were a few things she would let slide by; if you didn't
bring up your more dubious thoughts and inexplicable actions,
if these weren't discussed, it was almost as if they hadn't happened; this meant that underneath her real existence there was
a subterranean and anxiety-producing growth where she felt

terribly alone and cramped; and then, gradually, she had revealed all of these repressed thoughts, she no longer knew
solitude, but she felt cleansed of these confused mental stir-
rings. Pierre gave her back all the secret moments of her life
that she confided to him and in doing so he clarified and
completed them—they became a part of both their lives.
[*L'Invitée,* p. 27]

This testifies to an extraordinarily close and satisfying
relationship but seems again to contain rather unhealthy
and sinister overtones of extreme dependency and lack
of self-assertion on the part of Françoise. When she
speaks of "before when Pierre used to intimidate her"
there is enough of a suggestion of menace to cast a slight
pall over this perfect communion. To have to tell another
person *everything* could be a form of slavery as well as
deliverance, and Françoise's account, while it exalts their
union, makes her sound nonetheless pathetically dependent on Pierre. To feel that nothing is true until one tells
it to another is perhaps part of the universal desire to
escape from fundamental solitude, but when carried to
this extreme it betrays an almost dangerously weak hold
on reality. Indeed, this inner lack of self-assurance and
confidence in the validity of her own truths is Francoise's
undoing.

There is more, which the development of the novel
will unfold. Françoise and Xavière attend the performance of Pierre's play in which he has the leading role
of Julius Caesar. Seeing him on the stage, Françoise feels
a great upsurge of love and a tie of identification. Her
reflections about their relationship, though romantic,
seem to be a trifle unhealthy in the manner in which the
couple obliterates the individuals. Françoise reflects: "It's
true that we are one," she thought, with a surge of love.
It was Pierre who did the talking, he was the one who

decided everything, but his attitudes and accents were as much a part of Françoise's life as hers were; or rather you could say there was only one existence at whose center it would be incorrect to put 'him' or 'me' but only 'us.' " (*L'Invitée,* p. 58) There follows a rhapsodic reverie which reveals in Françoise a passionate belief in the possibility of permanence in love; in short she regards Pierre and herself as an eternal couple, united forever. Now, what is this really but a romantic conception of marriage? In its exalted and lyrical tone it is in fact the absolute antithesis of the cynical picture of marriage which emerges from *The Second Sex.* These are her reflections:

> Pierre was on stage and she was in the audience, but nevertheless it was the same play that was being acted in the same theatre. Their life together was like that; they didn't always see it from the same angle; through their separate moods, desires and pleasures each one would discover a different aspect of it: it was none the less the same life. Neither time nor distance could divide them; no doubt there were scenes, ideas and faces which had existed independently of the couple at first, but they reassembled these scattered instants into a unique whole where yours and mine became indistinguishable. Neither of them would ever appropriate even the smallest parcel of these privileged moments for himself alone; that would have been the worst treason. The only one. [*L'Invitée,* p. 59]

For a woman who feels this way the experiment of the trio might well be a strain! The passionate insistence that she and Pierre constitute "a unique entity" and the possessiveness and jealousy implicit in "the worst betrayal" indicate that the enlightened rationalism of the trio does not go very deep. This particular emotional outburst sets the stage for the subsequent conflict in Françoise.

Pierre, Françoise, and Xavière spend long and mildly

bibulous evenings together in cafés and have interminable but quite engaging conversations where all sorts of subtle cross-currents are constantly operating. Pierre takes an evident interest in Xavière, charmed by her youthful intensity, and even by her arbitrary sullenness and moodiness. Françoise too is charmed by her, alternately touched and annoyed by her vulnerability and her childish capriciousness, but all the same a certain "malaise" begins to poison her thoughts. As usual she and Pierre discuss everything afterwards, and they speculate about Xavière's feelings and meticulously analyze her every word and gesture. They even discuss the possibility of Pierre's becoming "amoureux." The following exchange between Pierre and Françoise indicates that Françoise is jealous but has to hide it; it also shows a rather fatuous egotism and curious male obtuseness in Pierre:

'To have an agreeable liaison with her I'd have to commit myself completely and I haven't the time nor the desire to.'
—'Why not the desire?', said Françoise. She had just felt a twinge of absurd jealousy; they told each other everything and never hid anything from each other: Pierre looked at her hesitatingly.
—'It doesn't annoy you that I suggest her having a love affair with me?'
—'Of course not,' said Françoise, 'Why do you ask?'
—'I don't know, you looked a little miffed. You like her a lot; you could want to be the main person in her life.'
—'You know perfectly well that she takes up rather too much of my time and energy.'
—'I know that you're never jealous,' said Pierre, smiling. 'Even so, if you ever were, even once, you should tell me. In this respect I'm rather like an insect—I have this mania for conquests but they really don't matter very much to me.'
'Naturally, I would tell you,' said Françoise. She hesitated.

entails cruelty and falseness masquerading as frankness. She does not say that this was the case with her and Sartre, however. Simone de Beauvoir describes this harmful "sincerity":

> If two speakers mutually persuade each other that they domi-
> nate the events and people about whom they are exchanging
> confidences, they are deceiving themselves. There is a kind of
> loyalty which I have observed which is only flagrant hypocrisy;
> confined to the domain of sexuality this "loyalty" doesn't
> really aim at creating a more intimate understanding but rather
> to provide one of them—most frequently the man—with an
> easy alibi—he deludes himself with the illusion that by confess-
> ing his infidelities he redeems them, whereas in fact he only
> inflicts a double pain upon his partner. [LFDL'A, pp. 29–30]

This is a profound observation, but Simone de Beauvoir and Françoise are presumably not subject to this form of hypocrisy. Simone de Beauvoir says: "No timeless rule can be relied on to make every couple perfectly honest with each other; it is for the people involved to decide what kind of relationship they want to have." Françoise chooses the hard path: "perfect sincerity" is exactly what she and Pierre believe is possible and think that they practice. However, the entire novel is an exquisite demonstration of the self-delusion of Françoise. She has a touching faith in reason and a need to believe in its efficacy, but the text depicts in minute detail how reason in human relationships is often a mere facade and how feelings dominate behavior and elude subjective analysis. "Le coeur a ses raisons que la raison ne connaît pas" has become trite by over-repetition, but it could serve all the same as an epigraph to this novel, as well as Hegel's somber phrase.

There is an episode where Pierre, jealous of Xavière,

Perhaps in all honesty, one would have to call this evening's malaise jealousy; she *hadn't* liked Pierre's taking Xavière so seriously; but it was a momentary moroseness which had a lot to do with sheer fatigue. If she told Pierre about it, instead of a fleeting unhappy mood it would become an unpleasant and sticky reality; he would have to make allowances for it himself in the future, whereas she didn't really admit its existence herself. It didn't exist; she wasn't jealous.
—'You can even fall in love with her if you want,' she said.
—'Oh, it isn't a question of that,' said Pierre. [*L'Invitée,* p. 79]

Innumerable variations on this scene occur, each one more oppressive and painful for Françoise than the last. She always must deceive herself, repress her jealousy, call it by another name and blandly assure Pierre that she is the understanding, magnanimous Françoise who is above jealousy. Here it is relatively benign, but these scenes later become almost unbearable. The human misunderstandings and mutual torture come ironically from the perfect accord and the agreement to be utterly honest; as a result truthfulness becomes derisive. Françoise can't tell the truth because she represses it in herself; their real thoughts are often miles apart. What if Françoise had said freely, "Yes, I am jealous." What would have happened? Would she have lost Pierre's esteem for this honest assertion?

In *La Force de L'Age* Simone de Beauvoir describes another "pact" between Sartre and herself: "Not only did neither of us ever lie to the other, but we never hid anything from the other." (LFDL'A, p. 28) She tells how this bothered her at first, having treasured her solitude and privacy but how finally this absolute honesty and total self-exposure was a source of supreme satisfaction. Nonetheless she subsequently discusses in a penetrating way how "perfect sincerity" can be an illusion and often whom he imagines to be sleeping with Gerbert, behaves in a shamefully petty way by creeping down the hall and trying to see if Gerbert is really in Xavière's room. This is a frightful experience for Françoise and Pierre. Afterwards, as usual they analyse Pierre's behavior: "you can't imagine how sordid I feel wandering the corridors in pajamas and spying through keyholes."—"I know quite well how sordid passion is," said Françoise. Her serenity was restored; Pierre no longer seemed monstrous to her since he was capable of judging himself lucidly." (*L'Invitée,* p. 382) This admiration for lucidity which redeems one's actions is pathetic since Pierre understands himself no better than Françoise does and much of this self-analysis is hollow verbalizing. Their rationalism blinds them to feelings which cannot be altered or explained away by talking lucidly about them. Françoise says that passion is sordid, but what Pierre feels for Xavièrte is so far removed from real passion that Françoise's neat wrapping up of reality in little comprehensible packages is a mockery of the real situation. If it were indeed real passion that Pierre feels the whole performance would be less weirdly equivocal and absurd.

Simone de Beauvoir creates an increasing crescendo of anguish in Françoise, who simultaneously feels growing jealousy and emptiness in herself. As she loses the conviction of Pierre's real love and need for her, she feels that she is drained of all her own character and force, so much has she depended on Pierre for her own identity. Xavière becomes a bone of contention and reveals the abyss between Pierre and Françoise, since they interpret her actions in totally different ways. Pierre returns from a tête-à-tête with Xavière, who had peevishly attacked Françoise's "moralism," Pierre's "seriousness", i.e., his devotion to his work, etc. He explores every nuance of these conversations with Françoise and transforms Xavière's childish petulance into the daring ability to live in the present, intensity of feeling, etc. Françoise sees egoism and amour-propre in Xavière while Pierre regards her as a marvel of freshness and verve, fiery in her scorn of mediocrity. Françoise bravely disagrees, but Pierre blithely goes on weaving rapturous images of this golden creature and Françoise has to endure it. He even finds Xaviere's rudeness to Françoise somehow delightful because her inability to get along with people seems so childlike and touching. Afterwards, Françoise reflects that "Every minute that we didn't spend with her we spent talking about her—she became an obsession." (*L'Invitée*, p. 163) And suddenly everything seems false, Pierre's interest in her a sham, mere gestures and words: the old reassurances fail her and she is overwhelmed with a sense of irreparable loss, although she absolves Pierre of all blame: "But it wasn't Pierre's fault. He hadn't changed. It was she who had for years made the mistake of regarding him only as a justification for herself." (*L'Invitée*, p. 164) What is so pathetic about Françoise's self-analysis is that she always heaps blame upon herself and exonerates the others who make her suffer. The reader often has the impression that Pierre, on the other hand, is a heartless, unimaginative male.

Indeed, what is unspeakably horrible is that Françoise not only feels jealousy but has invested so much of her life in Pierre that her sense of her own worth is absolutely undermined. If Pierre can feel this way about Xavière, doesn't that mean that Francoise has failed him, or that he never really loved her, or that she lacks the requisite qualities? Her whole sense of self evaporates because she cannot capture Pierre's all-encompassing interest. Here jealousy is indeed soul-destroying because the self depends utterly upon what others think and feel. For example, the trio are at a party. Françoise observes Pierre's and Xaviere's rapt absorption in each other and is led to make despairing philosophical reflections on her self.

'Who am I?' she wondered; she looked at Xavière whose face shone with shyly worshipping admiration; women like that, everybody knew who they were. . . . 'I'm nobody,' thought Françoise; . . . And yet Xavière judged her, she compared her with Paule; which of them would she prefer? She turned to look at Pierre but he wasn't looking at her; his gaze was fixed on Xavière; with her mouth open and her eyes misted over, Xavière was having trouble breathing; she no longer knew where she was; she seemed far away; Françoise looked away with annoyance; Pierre's concentration was indiscreet and almost obscene; the face of this possessed creature was not something to be displayed in public. At least Françoise was capable of knowing that she couldn't experience passionate trances like that. She could know with a good deal of conviction what she was not; it was very painful though to only know oneself as a series of negative possibilities.
'Did you see Xavière's expression?'
—'Yes,' Françoise said. He had uttered these words without taking his eyes off Xavière.
—'That's how it is,' Françoise thought. She didn't possess any distinctive traits for him any more than for herself; invisible, indistinct, she was a part of him; he talked to her as though he were talking to himself, but his glance remained glued to Xavière. [*L'Invitée*, p. 164]

Without doubt Simone de Beauvoir is playing on certain chords from *L'Etre et Le Néant* in her description of the "vide" in Françoise, her nothingness, etc., but Françoise's self-denigration does reveal a lack of self-esteem that is the root of her suffering. She finally breaks down, weeps, and reproaches Pierre. With real apparent anguish and concern he assures Françoise that his interest

in Xavière must not in any case damage *their* relationship
and he will immediately renounce all claim to Xavière if
it wounds Françoise, but Françoise still cannot utter a
word. She experiences the terrible human realization that
one cannot force the emotions of another and it is what
one feels, not what one says, that matters. After a sulking
scene by Xavière, Françoise looks at Pierre and suffers
some more, because she knows intuitively that Xavière
does attract Pierre despite all his noble allegations to the
contrary; the least pout from Xavière upsets him more
than all of Françoise's "existential" suffering. This impossible and mutually destructive impasse continues to
wrack the characters for another hundred and fifty pages,
becoming more and more involuted with Gerbert's absorption in the group. Basically, however, nothing new
is added to the division in Françoise and the complexities
of her relation with Pierre. The poignancy of her suffering is manifest and the drama of her total submission to
Pierre, despite her intelligence and courage, drives the
novel to its fateful end.

The anguish of Françoise provides an interesting commentary on *The Second Sex* written several years later. In
the chapter called "Woman's Situation and Character"
Simone de Beauvoir admits that women do have many
weaknesses and that "the indictments brought against
women from the Greeks to our own time" are in fact
based on solid evidence, but that these weaknesses are
not inherent but due to woman's "situation." She obviously has to take account of infinite variety in character,
but she does suggest that women are indeed less admirable than men. They have been forced into immanence
and passivity which are not productive of the highest
human traits. Women are forced to be coquettes and to
play guilefully upon men's sexual feelings because their

whole existence depends upon pleasing men. Their enforced dependency promotes feminine wiles and
manipulation which is a form of revenge against men for
the fact that their entire lives are spent waiting for and
on *them.* Since their sole justification rests on male approval, women develop the bad, falsely ingratiating
qualities that slaves and underlings always have. Outwardly Françoise is the absolute antithesis of the co-
quette. She scorns the kind of petty manipulation and
dishonesty that coquettishness implies, and is steadfastly
open and frank. Yet, ironically, in spite of the superficial
difference in character traits, this view of woman's life
applies to Françoise too. She reproaches herself over and
over for having made Pierre the "justification of her
existence." Though she never contemplates breaking
with Pierre, she is bitter that her existence depends upon
him. Despite Françoise's individuality and her obvious
rejection of the traditional feminine roles of wife and
mother or mistress economically dependent on her
lover's constancy, this description fits her as well as the
women *The Second Sex* has in mind: "She expects to find
her raison d'être, her value and her very being from
them [men]."

Of course, the themes of *The Second Sex* do not necessarily have to be reflected in Simone de Beauvoir's novels, particularly *L'Invitée,* which predates *The Second Sex*
by six years. However, one can note that the novelist is
perhaps the better psychologist and intuitively grasps the
human complexities that evade the theoretician and
polemicist. For if one were to use Françoise as a model,
one might refute, or at least modify significantly, the
major thesis of *The Second Sex,* which is that only by being
economically independent can a woman achieve "firm
inner freedom." Françoise is economically independent;

she does not live for or through her husband and children, and yet her whole crisis stems from a too profound dependency on another human being. Economic independence may be a necessary, but it is not a sufficient cause of real freedom. Further more, Francoise's character is not traditionally feminine, in the sense of being fluttery, docile, and domestic science-bound; she has cultivated all of her gifts of originality and intelligence, and yet she is prey to extreme emotional fragility. The novel would seem to imply that dependence is a much more complicated concept than *The Second Sex* allows since all human relations necessarily involve it; it therefore cannot always mean reprehensible weakness and humiliation unless one regards all human relations as being an intolerable infringement on human freedom.[8]

The example of Françoise in no way undermines Simone de Beauvoir's conviction that economic independence for women is a great and final good, but other ideas of *The Second Sex* are harder to extract from *L'Invitée*. To be sure, Simone de Beauvoir has not yet invented the theory, but Françoise is feminine and we have the right to examine her through *The Second Sex*'s binoculars. Her character is hard to account for strictly in terms of "woman's situation." All of the characters have their strengths and weaknesses, charm and perversity, and the question of sex seems somewhat irrelevant. Xavière is a hare-brained young girl, dependent on Pierre and Françoise; she cannot even summon up enough force and self-discipline to find a métier, and yet she is able to dominate both Pierre and Françoise. Although in some ways pathetic and weak, she also has the strength of character to be resolutely what she is and to impose herself on others. The contrary of the ideal of *The Second Sex,* she exhibits much more force and independence of character than Françoise, who better embodies their ideal.

The Second Sex continually regards dependence, passivity, and weakness as automatically being moral flaws, not conducive to admirable human behavior; although it is extremely vague in its use of these terms, they are regarded as being demeaning, to be feared like the plague. Ironically though, in spite of her dependence, Françoise is also the most morally admirable person in the book. Dependence makes her suffer but does not seem to entail moral inferiority in any notable way (leaving out the drastic conclusion). In fact, the other characters are all more egotistical, assertive, aggressive, and hence less sensitive to others. Thus *The Second Sex* viewed through the perspective of Françoise and Simone de Beauvoir in the autobiography assumes interesting new dimensions, because one cannot help feeling that the extreme horror of passivity, weakness, dependence, and "immanence" that give the work its special emotive tone expresses in some way Simone de Beauvoir's reaction against a strong dependent streak in herself. Like all thinkers, she has subconsciously, in an ultimately mysterious and unfathomable way, erected a theory partly from her observations and convictions, but also from her inner emotional necessities.

In my opinion *L'Invitée* intuitively wrestles with some of these ambiguities and contradictions. Though as a work of art it provides no answers, it shows in an imaginatively provocative way the hollowness of reason as an absolute or a panacea in human relations and suggests indirectly that sincerity or generosity are not to be had through an act of reason or will. In the last analysis it would seem to be the spontaneous quality of feelings themselves which determines their sincerity, which no amount of ratiocination can alter. In addition, the dedication to absolute freedom and individual self-fulfillment can also mean devastating egoism, ruthlessness, and cruelty. Françoise's dependency or weakness, however painful for her, make her more humanly and morally attractive than Pierre with his self-confessed "imperialism" or Xavière with her vaunted amorality.

Françoise can be regarded as a significant milestone in Simone de Beauvoir's theory of woman. Appearing in a novel before the evolution of the theory, she displays, if only in a negative way, many of Simone de Beauvoir's basic attitudes on this subject. She is economically independent, but emotionally passive and thus demonstrates that economic independence may be a necessary but not a sufficient cause of a liberated personality. Furthermore, Françoise is not a "positive" heroine because of her dependency and weakness. She reflects Simone de Beauvoir's own unresolved problems, before she had fully formulated her doctrine of "woman's fate." Let us see then, what Simone de Beauvoir will do later with another heroine likewise modeled after herself, but who was created after the author had thoroughly cogitated the implications of *The Second Sex*. This heroine is Anne Dubreuilh of *Les Mandarins*.

NOTES

1. Maurice Merleau-Ponty, "Le roman et la métaphysique," *Sens et Non-Sens,* ed. Nagel (Paris, 1948), 12:50–81.

2. Hazel Barnes, *Humanistic Existentialism: the Literature of Possibility,* (University of Nebraska Press, 1959), pp. 121 ff.

3. Georges Blin, "Simone de Beauvoir et le problème de l'action," *Fontaine,* no. 45 (Oct. 1945), pp. 716–30.

4. When Françoise kills Xavière, she is certainly "living" the philosophy

of *L'Etre et Le Néant*—at the expense of psychological versimilitude. A "metaphysical" murder is difficult to reconcile with a realistic novel. *L'Invitée* might be quite profitably examined for the way in which it calls into question some of the more extreme positions of *L'Etre et Le Néant.*

5. Blin.

6. This "dependence" of Françoise provides material for reflection on Simone de Beauvoir's militant stand in *The Second Sex.* It might indicate that the extreme fear of dependence in that work does indeed spring from Simone de Beauvoir's own experience and suffering.

7. As J. G. Weightman observes, "Another way, however, of seeing a pattern in the book would be to say that after she lost faith in her father's character and intelligence, she was looking for a man who could provide her with the relief of a masculine ideal. In this respect she was more feminine —and—dare we say so, perhaps more submissively bourgeoise, than might first appear. The milestones in her story are the men she looked up to and who turned out to be weaker and less intelligent than herself." J. G. Weightman, "Growing up in Paris," *Encounter* 13, no. 2 (Aug. 1959):77–81.

8. One can imagine a woman totally dependent upon a man economically who nevertheless, unlike Françoise, would have enough gumption to oppose her husband's ideas, for instance. Françoise is almost pathologically unable to oppose anything Pierre says, which suggests a serious flaw in the equation of economic and emotional independence.

3

Anne of
Les Mandarins

Anne Dubreuilh, heroine of *Les Mandarins,* is Simone de Beauvoir's only really "positive" heroine. Also, like Françoise, she is largely autobiographical, reflecting the author's character and experience. However, she too falls short of the emancipated ideal of *The Second Sex* and does not exemplify independence and firm control of one's destiny. In fact, she belongs to the category of "l'amoureuse" so rigorously analyzed in *The Second Sex.* The importance of love in woman's life looms large in Simone de Beauvoir's works. The feminine characters in the novels all place an extreme value on love and are ultimately dependent on men; none are embattled feminists who transcend their sex and claim equal rights in a masculine world. In *The Second Sex* Simone de Beauvoir devotes considerable attention to woman's erotic life. She describes how women, excluded from the masculine world of action and achievement, have often sought ways to justify their "relative" being by frankly exalting their femininity and reveling in the very limitations it presents.

One of these ways is that of "l'amoureuse". The bitter dilemma of woman who overestimates love because she does not have other sufficiently absorbing passions seems profoundly rooted in custom and feminine psychology.

Simone de Beauvoir quotes the old saws: "The word 'love' doesn't have at all the same meaning for one sex as for the other and that is the source of the serious misunderstandings which divide the two sexes. Byron said accurately that in man's life love is only a part-time occupation whereas for woman it is her whole existence." (TSS, II, p. 603) By "l'amoureuse" Simone de Beauvoir means the woman who has defiantly dedicated her entire life to love. She admits that there is a certain tragic grandeur about this desperate measure. She describes, for instance, the pathetic existence of Juliette Drouet, Hugo's mistress, whose life was "only endless waiting around" and whose 17,000 letters to Victor Hugo testify to a sad dearth of meaningful occupation. But since abandonment and the death of love are always possible, if not inevitable, such total immersion in one's sentimental life is folly and delusion, unproductive and egocentric. "There are few crimes which exact a worse punishment than this generous fault: to put oneself entirely in another's hands and thus be at the other's mercy." (TSS, II, p. 628) Here again Simone de Beauvoir emphasizes the traditional dependence of woman; "l'amoureuse" seeks to glorify it, but with disastrous results since her total absorption in another becomes a tyrannical burden for the other. The examples given strike one as being somewhat dated since they are mostly drawn from periods when women *were* totally dependent on men and such strategy had more logic when the alternatives were so depressingly limited. Yet as a psychological attitude it still persists, and perhaps most women are temperamentally prone to this dangerous delusion. (The alternatives are *still* rather depressingly limited too, as we are learning.)

In addition, however, Simone de Beauvoir's discussion of "l'amoureuse" contains some ambiguities which are quite constant in her work. She herself always exalts love and continually stresses its power and importance; *Le Deuxième Sexe* gives inordinate attention to woman's affective life. At the beginning of the chapter Simone de Beauvoir, with examples from novels and journals, proves the eternal commonplace that love has the power to transform life; it is wondrous, magical, and indispensable to happiness. What she wants to decry is not love as such but a feminine wallowing in love; a tendency toward submissiveness and reliance on man which strikes her as demeaning and weak. The difficulty here is that in her global inclusion of every possible male-female relationship and in her lyrical flights about "l'amoureuse", she is also often describing the peculiar madness of love itself common to everybody. "L'amoureuse" is thus sometimes just an exaggerated case of the ordinary woman in love; the behavior that Simone de Beauvoir regards as blamable is characteristic of the way all people feel (if they have an ounce of imagination) when they're victims of this emotion. Madness, perhaps, but this marvelous feeling creates at least an illusion of rare human sympathy and understanding. Here is Simone de Beauvoir on women in love:

> The supreme goal of human love, as of mystical love, is identification with the loved one. The measure of values, the truth of the world, are in his (the lover's) consciousness; hence it is not enough to serve him. The woman in love tries to see with his eyes; she reads the books he reads, prefers the pictures and the music he prefers; she is interested only in the landscapes she sees with him, in the ideas that come from him; she adopts his friendships, his enmities, his opinions; when she questions herself, it is his reply she tries to hear ... [TSS, II, pp. 613–14]

Certainly this attempt at identification with the other is characteristic of women in love, although the somewhat servile tone of this passage with its spineless self-efface-ment before HIM, might elicit well-deserved feminist scorn. It well describes Simone de Beauvoir in her au-tobiography where she practically reenacts this passage; e.g., the long accounts of her total accord with Jean-Paul Sartre. But is it reprehensible surrender?

At the end of the chapter on "l'amoureuse" Simone de Beauvoir considers "authentic" love which is of course a "beautiful ideal." She defines it glowingly but in rather vague terms: each person being equally free, "neither one would relinquish his self-transcendence, neither would be maimed." For both people this love will mean an enrichment of the self and of the entire world. How-ever, Simone de Beauvoir returns to her fundamental thesis and insists that this kind of reciprocity is not possi-ble today, because woman is not free economically and therefore she will be dependent on a man and hence at his mercy. She quotes Nietzsche and Balzac, who lyri-cally glorify woman's capacity to love and give freely of herself, which is of course her raison d'être. Simone de Beauvoir observes wryly that while this is all very beauti-ful, it is really a cruel mystification since no man really wants or needs this kind of total devotion. In fact, it becomes a bore and a kind of slavery for the man. She concludes that only when woman is strong and free (not dependent economically) will love be for her, as for the man, "a source of life and not of mortal danger." Falling in love has always involved "mortal danger," because at that moment two people are necessarily "dependent" upon each other. Yet, like much in *The Second Sex,* there is a large kernel of truth in de Beauvoir's critique of "l'amoureuse", because women do depend excessively upon emotional attachments and are in many ways at the mercy of men.

The Second Sex is certainly a bewildering book. One often has the impression that Simone de Beauvoir herself shares in some degree the very attitudes she is deploring. Man is always such an enviable creature—strong, autonomous, independent, resourceful, energetic, etc. Perhaps *The Second Sex* would make cheerful reading for men, so insistent and unwavering is its overestimation of the male. Yet throughout the entire chapter Simone de Beauvoir has excoriated the absurd glorification and overestimation of the love object (the male) characteristic of "l'amoureuse," who regards her lover as "god," "idol," "hero," etc. This overestimation of the love object is of course a chief ingredient in romantic love, but "l'amoureuse" permanently attempts to entertain this illusion.

Simone de Beauvoir cites innumerable swooning, self-abasing avowals of women in love, such as: "A young woman will write: 'When will he come, he who can dominate me?' And when he comes, she will love to sense his manly superiority." (TSS, II, p. 607) Though the examples are chosen to demonstrate the absurdity of feminine self-immolation and servile worship of god-like masculine superiority, they faintly resemble the feelings of the young Simone de Beauvoir when she dreamed of the man she would one day meet and reminiscent of her comments about Sartre's being the only man who could ever dominate her intellectually. One often has the impression that Simone de Beauvoir shares, to a marked degree, many of the emotional attitudes associated with traditional "feminine psychology", but that for some reason she regrets these in herself, which accounts for the violence of her reaction in *The Second Sex*.[1]

However it may be, Simone de Beauvoir unequivocally censures "l'amoureuse" and concludes that her choice of life is tragically mistaken, condemning her to unhappiness and sterility, since she lives "through" another. Though this position is somewhat undermined by the preponderent weight Simone de Beauvoir gives to love in *The Second Sex,* it is her official position. It is with this negative "amoureuse" in mind that I shall examine the character of Anne in *Les Mandarins.* For if she is not an "amoureuse" in the pejorative sense of *The Second Sex,* she does nevertheless experience love in such a total way that her whole life is perilously affected by it. That is, she demonstrates what *The Second Sex* tends to gloss over: namely, that love is a powerful force to be reckoned with and cannot always be subordinated to the more important claims of career, etc. Anne's career and enlightened good sense do not protect her from the ravages of love. The case of Anne seems to indicate a certain gap between Simone de Beauvoir's rationalist ideal of sturdy feminine independence and the insoluable realities of the human condition. Of course, *The Second Sex* does not condemn love, but wants woman to place it in its proper subsidiary perspective as men do; yet Simone de Beauvoir celebrates Anne's love affair and it is as "l'amoureuse" that Anne's experience is memorable.

Les Mandarins is a long novel about a group of intellectuals and writers in Paris after the war. It deals with their personal, political, and ideological tribulations, and especially with their disillusion when the postwar world fails to fulfill their aspirations, which the exhilarating experience of fraternity in the Resistance had nourished. The novel has a certain imbalance because, while the main plot involves all the central figures in coherent and plausible relationships, several chapters are brusquely interposed to give a vivid and moving account of Anne Dubreuilh's love affair in America. The love affair is based on the experience of Simone de Beauvoir and in her autobiography she justifies this inclusion on the grounds that it reveals Anne's inner self more fully, and also because she enjoyed doing it. She states that it simply gave her much pleasure to transpose a personal experience that had affected her strongly into a novel and so she did it. Following some very sound criticism from Sartre she had tidied up the plot considerably, but she must leave in the love affair. Her artistic instincts were sound, for although the love affair does in a way mar the unity of the novel, it also produces its chief emotional impact.

Simone de Beauvoir explains that for Anne she has utilized much of her own experience and some of her own characteristics and feelings, but she has made a fictional character who is also a pure creature of the imagination, designed to fit the artistic exigencies of this particular novel. With *The Second Sex* behind her, Simone de Beauvoir is now consciously preoccupied with the peculiar difficulties of the feminine condition and all of her female characters reflect this. She remarks about Anne: "I assigned one of the important parts to a woman, because many of the things that I wanted to express were connected with my feminine condition." (LFDL'A, p. 284) However, though Anne has a profession—she is a psychiatrist—and is therefore literally an independent woman according to the dicta of *The Second Sex,* Simone de Beauvoir declares that she has made her a "dependent" woman in that she lives for others and her own ambitions are modest and secondary. This dependence makes her typically feminine and permits her to be a good observer and reflecting conscience. It enables her to comment on the main action presided over by the male protagonists with a degree of detachment and a different perspective. In short, she can be the author's voice.

Anne's profession remains in the background. She is a passive but articulate and sensitive observer while the center of the stage, which seethes with action, drama, and power, is occupied by men—all writers and all furiously "engagés". She shares their concerns and lavishes sympathy where needed. However, she is not really deformed by this dependence and cannot be said to live altogether vicariously through others or prey on their lives in the unwholesome way so pitilessly delineated in *The Second Sex.* Simone de Beauvoir says, "In Anne dependency was mitigated by the warmth and immediacy of the concern she displayed towards people and things." (LFDC, p. 284) In fact, here Simone de Beauvoir seems to show a curiously imprecise conception of "dependence," since Anne was deemed "dependent" at first because the center of her life was others, while here her dependence is "mitigated" because of her warm and direct interest in other people. This unresolved convergence of altruism and dependence is at the heart of Simone de Beauvoir's thesis about woman and must be dealt with later in more detail.

To what extent does Anne resemble her creator? Simone de Beauvoir offers her opinion on this question in the spirit of aggressive candor which is a salient feature of the autobiography:

'Could Anne be me then?' Of course, I gave her some of my traits, but I've explained why I created a creature in whom I don't recognize myself. I lent her tastes, feelings, friendships and memories which were mine and often my words were her words. Nevertheless, she didn't have my appetites nor my stubbornness nor above all the autonomy which a profession gives me and which I value so much. Her relations with a man twenty years older are almost filial and in spite of their close understanding they leave her solitary and lonely; she is only half-heartedly committed to her profession. Lacking personal projects and goals she leads the "relative" life of a "secondary being. [LFDC, p. 288]

Simone de Beauvoir apparently regards herself as one woman who has escaped the bondage of "relative life". Her explanation of why she makes Anne "dependent" while she herself is not is somewhat unsatisfactory. Why must Anne lack the autonomy which a profession that she values could give her? Here is Simone de Beauvoir's chance to give us a positive heroine according to her precepts and her example, and she muffs it. This remains the great enigma. It could suggest unresolved uncertainty in Simone de Beauvoir either about her own independence or her theory.

According to Dominique Aury, the male characters and the political and ideological conflicts of *Les Mandarins* are somewhat lifeless and occasionally monotonous —"People talk, talk, talk." But she says it is the singularity of the feminine characters and the love relationships that give the novel its tone and force.[2] This is a judicious estimate and Anne as the most important feminine character serves as a foil to all the rest. Despite her significant human weaknesses, she is kind and generous and possesses an outward serenity and self-possession that the other women sadly lack. They are well-drawn examples of what Simone de Beauvoir regards as the malediction of the female condition: in general, either sad little waifs or vengeful furies, bursting with fictional vitality. Anne is often the strong and reassuring mother-figure (after all, she is a psychiatrist), and she comforts and supports Paule, Henri's distraught mistress, and Nadine, her tempestuous and neurotic daughter. With them she exudes calm sympathy; they lean on her and value her judgment.

Anne, thirty-nine years old, is the wife of Robert Dubreuilh, who is twenty years older and a celebrated writer. In a flashback she gives her self-portrait and history up to the present; it is almost identical with that of Simone de Beauvoir as revealed in the autobiography. Anne is a psychiatrist and practices this profession; at the same time like Françoise she has a strong sense of her own inadequacy; she is self-effacing and not ambitious. Though on the surface her life is a successful one, she is full of self-reproach for her lack of self-assertion. Yet she also reassures herself that this existence is right for her, although her way of describing herself is so extremely self-denigrating that her rationalizations are not entirely convincing. Here are her inebriated musings during a Christmas party: "Why am I always so concerned with other people? I could just as well pay a little attention to myself. I lean my cheek against my pillow; I'm there, that's me; what's annoying is that I don't find anything to think about [this is decidedly *not* Simone de Beauvoir]. Oh, if someone should ask me who I am, I could show them my index file." (LM, p. 30) Then, ironically, with a good-natured jab at psychoanalysis, she lists all her dark declivities; couched in Freudian terms we have the record of Simone de Beauvoir's life from *Mémoires d'une Jeune Fille Rangée* on: strife with her mother, therefore difficulty with her (fictional) daughter, Catholic education, puritanism, loss of faith, marriage to a man she looks up to, "I was discovered to have a rather pronounced Oedipus complex which explains my marriage with a man twenty years older"; she and Robert are left-wing intellectuals, etc. Anne muses about herself in this way:

"Nothing about all this is completely inaccurate. Here I am, then, plainly catalogued and accepting it, adjusted to my husband, to my profession, to life and death, to the world and its horrors. That's me, me exactly, that's to say, nobody." (LM, p. 31) Of course she has drunk too much, which is a rather hoary novelistic device to fill one in on a character's past, but for a psychiatrist to say "just me, that's to say, nobody" seems surprising. "Nobody" is an extreme way of putting personal modesty, but Simone de Beauvoir has lent Anne her own extremism. Anne continues, converting her very lack of forcefulness into a kind of asset and showing the not too delicate hand of Simone de Beauvoir the polemicist on the woman question here. Anne becomes a classic case of a woman finding excuses for not running the world, not being a "grand aventurier" and making withdrawal a virtue. Here is Anne consoling herself:

> To be nobody, that is, in short, a privilege. I watched them all coming and going through the studio, all those who had achieved names or distinction for themselves, and I didn't envy them. Of course, Robert's pre-eminence had been pre-ordained, he was born a genius; but the others, how did they dare? How can one be arrogant or giddy enough to expose oneself with the common herd to a pack of unknown readers? Their names are soiled on a million lips, the curious pick their brains, their feelings and their lives; if I had handed my secret thoughts to these grasping rag-pickers, the public, they'd have been misunderstood and have been transformed into ordinary junk. I congratulated myself on being a nobody. [LM, p. 31]

Much later on Anne attends a political meeting where Robert receives a wild ovation. At this moment she is somewhat wistful about the power he represents. It is apparent that her excessive modesty is partly evasion and

rationalization of timidity rather an authentic choice.
Anne recounts the history of her love for Robert, who
had so overwhelmed her with his brilliance and passionate curiosity in her youth that she has always looked up
to him with respect bordering on awe: "From the moment I knew I loved him, I followed him enthusiastically
from surprise to surprise. I learned that you can live
without furniture or time schedules and how to do without lunch, to stay up all night, to sleep in the afternoon
and to make love in the woods as well as in bed." (LM,
p. 46) Now, however, the rapture is gone though there
remains profound affection. One senses that Anne is outwardly cheerful and energetic but that she is at a critical
age and quite melancholy because she is actually starved
for love. In short she is ripe for a love affair. There is a
nostalgic and elegiac tone in her reveries about the exuberance and gaiety of the past that conveys much more
than she expresses about her present mood. She maintains that her life is full: "Sexual desire between us had
faded away years ago; but we were too closely united for
the physical relationship to have too much importance;
by recognizing this fact we had not really lost anything."
(LM, p. 47)

Simone de Beauvoir expresses this half-submerged,
ill-defined yearning of Anne's in subtle ways. Mixed with
the vague malaise of a woman who feels that youth and
last chances for love are irrevocably slipping from her—
the universal anguish of middle age—is Anne's own peculiar and distinct "memento mori" temperament which
has a pronounced predilection for dwelling on death and
bodily decay. She seems to cultivate her morbid thoughts
and shows a trace of relish in this kind of reflection. Anne
is thus humanly poignant since inevitable old age and
final renouncement of love are part of the sadness of life,

but her own excessive preoccupation with decay and death are peculiar to her. It may appear at odds with her cheerfulness but the author makes it convincing. One evening at a party Anne recounts: "I went up to the buffet and had a glass of wine. My glance traveled down the length of my black skirt and stopped at my legs; no one had noticed my legs for ages, not even I; they were slender and confident under their covering of amber silk and they were just as nice as other women's legs; one day they would become dust without having ever really existed; that seemed unfair. I was absorbed in their contemplation when Scriassine came over to me." (LM, p. 32) These short reflections of Anne convey volumes about her not fully articulated melancholy. When Scriassine arrives at this moment it is an apt juxtaposition of events since Anne shortly thereafter succumbs to Scriassine's cold, calculating, and almost disinterested amorous advances. The scene is described in a chilling and unpleasant way although not without its macabre comedy since Scriassine reveals an absurd mixture of anxiety, detachment, and male amour-propre. This experience demonstrates that Anne is incapable of cynical, hygienic love affairs and that she is really profoundly romantic. What she finds especially revolting about Scriassine is the hostility in his eyes. For her love must include "tendresse."

In many ways Anne is a good existentialist and it is indeed striking how often her feelings of nothingness, fear of dying, and sense of the vanity of human endeavor reappear all through Simone de Beauvoir's own autobiography."[3] At fifteen in a sudden revelation Simone de Beauvoir loses her faith, which had been quite firmly implanted in her by a Catholic education, a devout mother, and her own ardent temperament. In this instant she experiences an extreme horror of death which will haunt her throughout her life. This is her account: "One afternoon in Paris I realized that I was condemned to death. What do other people do? What will I do? It seemed to me impossible to spend the rest of my life with my heart constricted with horror. When disintegration draws near, I wondered, when you are already thirty or forty and you think, "It will happen tomorrow," how can you stand it? More than death itself I dreaded this fright which would soon be my lot forever." (MD'UJFR, p. 113) This obsession with death lingers with Simone de Beauvoir all her life and she attributes to Anne an identical adolescent experience. Closely related is the sense of the vanity and absurdity of life which ceaselessly unfolds in an endless series of meaningless moments, all empty of significance because of the fact of death. Simone de Beauvoir describes a crisis of her late adolescence when she indulged in "le nouveau mal du siècle" very fashionable among literary figures of the period. She mocks her juvenile excesses of despair which certainly contained large amounts of self-dramatization and youthful romantic posturing, but these somber feelings do recur throughout her life and even become embedded in a philosophy which suits her temperament. Anne too is afflicted with a sense of the nothingness of life and given to sudden reflections on the vanity of things. She is outwardly "resigned" but inwardly burns with rage that life has to be the drab way it is, and the daily round inspires her with metaphysical horror. Anne is subject to secret thoughts of this nature ("might as well turn on the gas") when she savors an all-or-nothing attitude about life which must be lived on her terms or lose all its flavor. The revolt against the ennui of existence is a familiar feature of Simone de Beauvoir's autobiography and especially pronounced in her youth. She constantly laments the mediocrity of people and the insufficiency of life and she finds the resignation of average mortals contemptible. Youth and the promise of some vague ecstatic future enthrall her, but for this reason she is the more appalled at the gloom and drab sameness of life of the uninspiring adults around her. She compares the monotony of adult existence to housework:

> I had always pitied adults for the monotony of their existence; when I realized that in no time at all it would become *my* lot I was filled with dread. Every day breakfast, lunch, dinner; then the dishes to be washed; all these hours which endlessly flowed away, leading nowhere; would I have to live like that? I formed a picture in my imagination which was so clear and so dreary that I can remember it to this day: a long row of gray squares stretching out toward the horizon, getting smaller according to the rules of perspective but all of them exactly identical and uniformly dull and insipid; those were the days, the weeks, and the years. (MD'UJFR, p. 101)

This passage, which is inspired by a memory of helping her mother wash the dishes one gloomy afternoon, can serve as a precocious intimation of both *The Second Sex* and the existentialist novelist, with the gray drabness of unending thankless household chores ultimately responsible for these two illustrious but related offsprings. In adults such sentiments are more ambiguous and do not attract the indulgence one feels for youthful ferocity and revolt against the humdrum. When Anne and the adult Simone de Beauvoir entertain such thoughts it is hard to know whether to regard them as existentialist revolt or puerile nihilism and self-pity. Sometimes one detects a certain pose in this attitude, a bit too archly gloomy and theatrical about the self as when Simone de Beauvoir calls her journals: "the daily dust of my life."

The most harrowing of Anne's negative feelings is her dread of old age. Given the conditions of her life the approach of old age is bound to cause distress, and the way Simone de Beauvoir connects Anne's feelings about age with her love affair and her sense of loss afterwards has a real tragic density of feeling that is beautifully evoked and altogether lacerating. But Anne's feelings about old age are also part of her existentialist sensibility, morbidly pronounced. Simone de Beauvoir reveals a similar attitude towards old age, both aghast at it and somehow disapproving of it as though it were something shameful. Old age begins very young according to Simone de Beauvoir and in *La Force des Choses* Simone de Beauvoir, though still bounding with amazing energy and bounce is given to saying things like: "Since my fall from my bicycle I was missing a tooth; the gap showed and I didn't intend to have it filled in; why bother? Anyway, I was old now, I was thirty-six." (LFDC, p. 21) or: "Forty years old. Forty-one. My old age was hovering over me getting closer. It was lying in wait for me at the bottom of my mirror. It stunned me to feel it creeping up on me at a relentless pace whereas nothing about me had anything in common with it." (LFDC, p. 185) *The Second Sex* is excruciating on the horrors of old age for women: "While man ages gradually, woman is abruptly robbed of her femininity; she's still young when she loses her erotic attraction and the fecundity from which she derives her chances for happiness and her justification in her own and society's eyes; she has to keep on living, deprived of any future for about half of her life as an adult." (TSS, II, p. 399) Simone de Beauvoir's description of the ravages of body and spirit that maturity and old age inflict on women is not recommended for cheerful bedside reading. It makes mass female suicide at forty sound sensible. For "the erotic object" as *The Second Sex* calls her, growing old is indeed an unmitigated disaster, since she is doomed to spend perhaps half of her life utterly without purpose or joy. "There remain many years left to live when one is forty years old." (TSS, II, p. 627) These attitudes are meant to demonstrate that the traditional role of woman is responsible for the dismal diminution of the second half of life which presumably need not be like this if women were not solely dependent on their femininity, their child-bearing function or their status as "erotic object." Yet it is remarkable how this same despair about old age or even middle age and a sense of the vanity and emptiness of life after forty are common to both Simone de Beauvoir and Anne.

Anne is tormented by a ghoulish vision of herself, helplessly caught in the grip of old age even before it arrives:

> A woman of thirty-nine, a woman of a certain age! . . . My old age is lying in wait for me, no way to escape it; already I could catch a glimpse of it in the corner of my mirror. . . . I lift up my hair and see white streaks which are no longer just a curiosity or a trace but the beginning: soon my head will acquire while I am still alive the color of my bones. The complexion of my face might still seem supple and fresh but from one moment to the next the mask is going to slip, baring the rhumy eyes of an old woman. The seasons keep refurbishing themselves, defeats and disasters can be repaired, but nothing can prevent my own decrepitude. (LM, p. 78)

She looks forward to seeing Lewis again but her age obsesses her. She reassures herself that when she sees him six months from now she won't have "aged a lot." She watches other women her age who dance and flirt and is horrified by the lack of dignity of those who try to act younger than they are. She refuses to dance, saying, "I'm too old," (she's thirty-nine!), and her friend Paule makes light of Anne's "complexes." Anne reflects further: "My brief elation at feeling joyously young was quickly dissolved. Glass mirrors are too indulgent: this was the real mirror, the faces of women my own age, with their flabby skin, indistinct features, mouths in a state of collapse, bodies whose flesh is unevenly distributed and sinks in strangely beneath their girdles. "These are the bodies of old women," I thought, "and I'm their age." (LM, p. 506) She seeks to be implacably honest and rid herself of comforting illusions, but in her view of these other women there is a certain lack of charity that is a bit chilling. No doubt these particular women are not especially admirable creatures, but this revulsion about their looks betrays the same attitudes Simone de Beauvoir shows in *The Second Sex* where aging women are indeed fatally diminished when they lose their youth and beauty. There as here Simone de Beauvoir in a way supports the very prejudices she denounces. As if woman's worth actually *were* her status as an "erotic object", and as if her sex, not her humanity, defined her. There's not much compassion in this vision of life which always exalts egoism, action, power, success, youth, beauty, and transcendence while scorning and fearing dependence, weakness, immanence, resignation (or acceptance), contemplation, repose. Anne is ruthlessly candid with herself, however, and she admits that her obsession with age and pretense at premature resignation is a kind of complicated ruse, and that at bottom she has the intransigent and absolutist spirit of the girl she once was. Indeed her absolutism is a significant part of this fierce attitude toward old age because she cannot bear the sense of any diminution or compromise:

I chose to be different from these too ripe ogresses; really, though, I had other ruses which were no better than theirs. I'm always quick to say: I'm finished, I'm old; in this way I cancel out the thirty or forty years that I still have to live, old and done for and full of regret for the vanished past; I can't be deprived of anything since I've already renounced it; there is more prudence than harshness in this attitude I take; at bottom it covers up an enormous lie: I deny old age by refusing its illusions and compromises. Beneath my skin which has lost its freshness, I affirm the survival of a woman with intact claims on life, who refuses all compromise and who scorns the pathetic aging hides of forty-year-old women. But this woman no longer exists and will never be rejuvenated, even by Lewis' embraces. [LM, p. 508]

This is a masterful rendition of the kind of whistling-in-the-dark game everyone plays in order to make the harshness of life bearable. But Anne's radical insistence on middle age as being without dignity or purpose—"the sad hides of forty-year-old women"—betrays a revolt against the universal human condition strangely at odds with *The Second Sex*'s rationalistic thesis that woman's satisfaction in life should, like man's, derive from her status as a human being and not depend upon mere sexual attraction and "female" embellishments. Actually both revolt and rationalism are evident in *The Second Sex* and all of Simone de Beauvoir's works, so that often her basic attitudes seem to be at war and yet at the same time complementary. Rational prescriptions for irrational human arrangements do not mesh well with metaphysical revolt against the human condition.

For Anne is also an intelligent and resourceful person who does have passionate feelings about the world and ideas. She is in no way enveloped in the frivolous and empty narcissism of some of the brilliantly etched scarifying feminine types who flit through the novel. She attends a soirée where she is surrounded by "femmes du monde" who are stunningly elegant, emit clichés, and exude boredom. Observing these vaguely dissatisfied but exquisitely gowned women, Anne also feels compassion, and here she is the contrary of the wretched and sad person who meditates on the nothingness of things. Here is the positive Anne who warms to the drama of life:

> . . . Neither Dudule, nor Lucie nor any of the dainty and polished young women who flocked around me ever treated each other with the least sincerity or affection. I felt a troubled pity for them. Their own lot was empty ambition, burning jealousies, abstract victories and defeats. And all the while there are so many things on earth to love and to hate passionately. Robert is so right. Indifference doesn't exist. Even in this milieu where it was hardly worth the effort I found myself seething with fierce opinions and moral indignation; I couldn't help reacting affirmatively to life and I knew quite well that nothing would extinguish my certain conviction that the world would always be full of things to love or to hate. [LM, p. 343]

Simone de Beauvoir succeeds in making Anne complicated and ambivalent, always vacillating a little in a human way about what she does finally feel about life. Her positive ardor about the sheer joy of existence conflicts with her morbid death-obsessed penchant but is somehow related to it since both attest to her passionate nature and hatred of mediocrity and indifference.

Anne is shown as a sympathetic wife who is solidly committed to Robert's career and his ideas; she treats him with infinite feminine tact and diplomacy and instinctively avoids trying to oppose his views too stridently or to impose her own. She "handles" him in the classic feminine way so much admired by men by ultimately deferring to him on ideological matters or by at least pretending to, sometimes reserving her own misgivings to herself when she disagrees with him as she does about the big issue which divides them all, the discovery of Stalin's concentration camps. At the same time, she lacks self-assertion and audacity and when the prospect of a trip to America presents itself she procrastinates and fears the adventure; Robert and Nadine need her; she cannot leave them, etc. She gradually realizes that she is not indispensable and healthy egoism carries the day. She will go to America.

As a mother Anne is exemplary since she has a daughter who would sorely try anyone's soul. Nadine is a fascinating neurotic creature, truculent and morose, capricious, uncompromising, and violently aggressive, who is obviously profoundly lacking in self-esteem. Her astonishing antics are at once captivating and appalling, and Anne's unruffled sympathy for her daughter's anguish is remarkable since Nadine often treats her mother with violent disrespect and surly hostility. Anne is both mother and psychiatrist with her daughter, and her acceptance of Nadine's behavior while gently attempting to dissuade her from her more self-destructive impulses demonstrates mellow wisdom. She recognizes that some of Nadine's troubles have their roots in the mother-daughter relationship, but she does not for that reason heap coals of guilt and self-reproach on her own head. Anne as mother, calm, somewhat detached, yet affectionate and Anne as an emotion-tossed woman in love are apparently two different people, but in reality the same affectionate nature which tries to imagine what the other feels is present in both, the difference being the ingredient of passion which has a way of unhinging the most tranquil.

Yet it is as "l'amoureuse" that Anne is memorable. It

is her love affair and her violent reaction to it that color the entire perception of her character. The chapters devoted to it are the most intense and Anne's consciousness dominates the entire novel so that her initial sadness, violent happiness in love, and subsequent despair and sense of loss are the main focus of her experience. Dominique Aury regards this episode as exceptional. She considers the love affair one of the best novelistic versions of a love affair from a woman's point of view: "Everything is in it: the sudden and rending revelation; the marvel of the first night of love; the flame of happiness; the ashes of separation; the agony of silence; alternating hope and despair, the ambiguity of reconciliations."[4] According to the same critic, the love affair is so well-rendered that the two principals have a vitality the other characters lack, and, paradoxically Lewis Brogan is the most successful and believable male character in the novel, "because Anne is in love with him." There is a small, delicious irony in the fact that Simone de Beauvoir, who exalts men because of their action, power, and adventurous spirit and who scorns women because they live for love and are creatures of the kitchen and the boudoir, should manage to make the outsider, an American even, more interesting than the other men who are importantly engrossed in momentous actions and the real world of politics and ideas—and this because he is a *lover.*

Anne as a woman in love has all the charms and failings of this bittersweet condition. She possesses the power of total recall and every insignificant detail is etched indelibly on her memory. She is impressed by the very dinginess of Brogan's apartment, his leather jacket, the linoleum on the floor, no frigidaire, and old mangy papers lying about. Decidedly, she is not a woman awed by wordly success and the pathetic squalor of Brogan's surroundings only accentuate his romantic glamour as an American writer at war with the crass American commercial success-mad society. Instantly he recognizes a kindred spirit as he apologizes for the mess in his apartment and speaks ironically of her elegant hotel, "the most beautiful in Chicago," which Anne scorns precisely for its boring, opulent, Hiltonian bad taste. Simone de Beauvoir recreates all the simultaneous anxiety and miraculous happiness of a love affair where two people who have been intensely lonely find each other and feel restored—the pure chance of their meeting seems fatefully necessary after the fact. Here Anne is without doubt "l'amoureuse," but all the pedantic distinctions in *The Second Sex* about women of this kind or that simply do not apply. She is instantly recognizable simply as a woman in love, and nothing can save her from this dreadful but glorious condition. Anne thinks with fright: "I have put myself completely in someone else's power. What madness!" but she goes on blithely to her own destruction the way lovers do. Lewis has disturbing inscrutable moods and silences Anne cannot fathom, but she dimly senses that they express his suffering because her necessary departure casts a pall on their precarious happiness. All the arid theorizing in *The Second Sex* about authentic, true reciprocal love being impossible until "that day when woman is free from her bondage," etc. strikes one as absurdly irrelevant here where two human beings discover that each is essential to the other's happiness. Two people fall in love in the usual way; this transforms their lives for a brief moment and nothing could save them from "the mortal danger" they freely embrace.

Anne, who is a self-effacing person, experiences the intoxicating feeling of being infinitely valuable, appreciated for her own sake and all without even trying.

"Nothing was expected of me: it was enough for me to be just what I was and a man's desire for me changed me into something rarely wonderful." (LM, p. 319) Simone de Beauvoir reproaches woman for finding her worth in what she is rather than what she does, for, according to the existentialist formula, "One only is what one does." But apparently in love it is what people *are,* not what they *do,* that counts. Lewis' attitude toward Anne is indulgently and mockingly affectionate; not that of the world which judges on outward merits and accomplishments— all those merit badges and silver cups. He says to Anne: "In the article you were called a brilliant doctor."— "That amazed you?" He looked at me without answering and smiled; when he smiled at me this way I felt as though I could feel his breath on my lips."—"I thought that they had pretty peculiar doctors in France." (LM, p. 315) Anne enjoys Lewis' astonishment at her professional renown, and even his faint mockery because it accentuates his exclusive interest in her as a human being and as a woman. She is characteristically feminine in her pleasure in being considered not "une femme de tête" but just herself, a woman and possibly just a little weaker, more dependent than Lewis. Absurd and regrettable according to *The Second Sex,* but Anne acts this way. Lewis has a bizarre circle of acquaintances, drug addicts, etc., and he and Anne are somewhat annoyed at the brusque intrusion of a strange woman claiming to be his fiancée; Anne finds that she is an escapee from a mental institution, one of the old "cases" he had befriended. Lewis explains: "Since I've lived here, weird things have happened. It's this place you see. It attracts cats, crazy people and drug addicts," He took me in his arms, "and the pure in heart." (LM, p. 326) Clearly Lewis has great charm and his protective manner of treating Anne reassures her.

With him she can be feminine, a bit submissive perhaps (as with Robert too), all generosity and tender sollicitude: the antithesis of a competent, aggressive, assertive, independent, emancipated woman. Lewis finds her softness charming. Love transforms the world and hideous Chicago becomes a delightful place, its tawdry ugliness full of magic. Lewis gives voice to the supreme quality of a "grand amour," unalloyed pleasure in another's happiness. As Anne relates: "We bought ham, salami, a bottle of chianti and a rum cake. We turned the corner of the street where the SCHLITZ sign shined red. At the foot of the stairs among the garbage cans he pressed me to him. 'Anne!' Do you know why I love you so much? It's because I make you happy.' " (LM, p. 323) Anne decides to stay two more weeks in Chicago though she realizes she is veritably taking her life in her hands. She knows that if she does stay, it will become a real love affair and impossible because of her other commitments and that she will suffer. She practices detachment and tries to think of Lewis as a man she has forgotten. This is sheer self-deception and false prudence; it's too late; impossible to think of Lewis as a man she has forgotten. As *The Second Sex* says, "A prudent woman in love—but these two words contradict each other." Anne is weak and succumbs but love is its own reward. At this moment she is "l'amoureuse" who feels her existence justified by love. However, this is not presented as a fault but as a generous weakness. Simone de Beauvoir the novelist manages to elicit our abiding conviction that love is indeed a great good and the very suffering it portends proves its irresistible power.

The agony of separation begins when Anne must return to Paris. She goes to her room to pack. Here she is:

It looked as if a mad killer had just murdered a woman and ransacked her closets and drawers. Actually it was the entrance to a funeral hall—all these objects were what remained of a dead woman; they were the provisions for the last trip she was going to take into the hereafter. Lewis came up to the chest of drawers, opened a drawer and took out a mauve box which he handed to me a little sheepishly.

—'I bought this for you.' Under the silky paper was a huge, white, fragrant flower. I took the flower, crushed it against my mouth and threw myself sobbing on the bed.

—'You don't have to eat it,' said Lewis, 'Do they eat flowers in France?' [LM, p. 330]

The funeral metaphors are apt correlations of Anne's feelings and Lewis' humorous little touch about the French eating flowers provides the last twist of the knife. The love affair will continue; Anne visits Lewis and travels with him in Mexico; she returns to spend a summer with him but finds he is no longer in love with her; and finally she returns to Paris and the painful realization that the affair is irremediably finished.

The pain Anne feels here at parting is revived over and over again. The salvation this love has brought entails in turn desolation and a sense of being only half alive when deprived of it. Anne carries on gallantly at Paris and attends to the daily affairs of her life, but this experience has a mortal effect on her. It is difficult to separate natural human grief from pathological fixation, and surely Anne's case is a delicate mixture of the two. Though she is an "amoureuse", she is not guilty of self-immolation. The misery she and Lewis both endure comes from the tragic nature of things—the relcalcitrance of time, chance, and distance to human desires and hopes—rather than from feminine dependency and avoidable weakness in Anne. The very artistic mastery that Simone de Beauvoir lavishes on this love affair exalts and celebrates

Anne's quality as "amoureuse." Here love is both "source of life" and "mortal danger" for the man and the woman.

The case of Lewis shows how a good novel obdurately resists simple theories. His total commitment to love contradicts the absurd simplifications about masculine freedom and insouciance endlessly proliferated in *The Second Sex*. Simone de Beauvoir says that even in a love which is mutual, there is a difference between the woman's and the man's feelings which the woman doesn't like to admit. It is impossible for a woman to find mutual dependence in the person she loves because she loves him for his very independence and strength. There is a paradox involved that women couldn't love men if they loved in the same way, because then the man would seem weak and dependent to the woman. (TSS, II, p. 621) In connection with Anne and Lewis this idea is sheer nonsense. The reason Lewis does finally end the affair is really due to his inability to accept a partial love and a woman he can only see at rare intervals. In the autobiography Simone de Beauvoir quotes a letter from Nelson Algren, the original model for Lewis Brogan, which explains how he felt that love must be all or nothing: "One can retain the feelings one has for someone," Algren wrote me, "but not accept any longer the fact that this person can control and upset one's whole life. Loving a woman who doesn't belong to you and who puts other people and things before you, without there ever being a chance that you could come first, is not acceptable." (LFDC, p. 270)[6] Before her final leave-taking Anne looks at Lewis and in a wave of sympathy she understands what he has suffered and why it is all over. It is clear that there is reciprocity of suffering in love. Furthermore, in this particular relationship Lewis has been the one with

the most to lose which in no way diminishes his man-
hood. Dependence on another is not necessarily a crime:

> Lying on his back in the dark he described the days and nights
> he had spent in this room alone, and my heart contracted. His
> life had seemed poetic to me, like the Indians' life seemed to
> Phillip, but for him, what a bare and lonely existence it had
> been! How many weeks on end without a single encounter or
> adventure or another living soul to talk to. How he must have
> wanted a woman who belonged to him completely! There had
> been a time when he thought that he might escape from this
> solitude; he had dared to risk falling in love. He had been
> disappointed, he had suffered and then he had recovered. [LM,
> p. 536]

Anne's attempt to recover from her love affair with
Lewis is given an ironic twist when she tries to comfort
Paule, Henri's mistress, whose unhealthy dependence on
love finally brings on a nervous breakdown. But Anne
privately reflects that she too regards love as all-impor-
tant and her morose exaltation of love at all costs reveal
her as a spiritual sister of Paule: "What will she be like
afterwards? [her cure] Oh, on the whole that's easy
enough to predict. She would be like me and millions of
other women: a woman who waits for death without
knowing any more why she is living." (LM, p. 420) This
is precisely the hopeless note of "l'amoureuse" in *The
Second Sex* when the savour of existence vanishes with
love, and life after forty is sterile and empty, a mere
waiting for death. Simone de Beauvoir takes great pains
to deplore this uncourageous attitude which expresses
sorrow at the evanescence and cruelty of life but which
is also weak self-indulgence and self-pity since no life can
escape loss, lack of love, loneliness, etc. Her theoretical
formulations about the self-defeating vanity of living

only for love are convincing, but her heroine Anne's reflections about the emptiness of life "sans amour" somehow undermine her positive affirmations. At any rate, Anne in these musings displays morbid leanings and a touch of romantic cosmic self-pity. Her robust good sense and native optimism are temporarily in eclipse.

The final chapter of *Les Mandarins* presents the crisis of Anne's life. She is drowning in an access of despair in which the necrophilic tendencies already noted overwhelm her. She is on the very brink of swallowing sleeping pills when the voices of her daughter and husband below restrain her and she rejoins the living, shaken, still feeling empty, but called back to life by the sense that others need her. Her broken love affair contributes to her distraught condition, but it is clear that Simone de Beauvoir intends Anne's would-be suicide as an expression of her exacting nature. In short it is an existentialist despair that Anne exhibits; her desperate act is not merely the banal woe of a woman at the end of a love affair, but a more philosophical despair. Simone de Beauvoir translates this fairly well into the kind of emotional collapse that a person contemplating suicide might have. It is not altogether convincing inasmuch as the metaphysical elements are a bit too intrusive; even Anne's spiritual malaise seems insufficient to account for this violent onslaught of numb despair. Anne looks at Robert tenderly but she is undone by gruesome thoughts about his death which she foresees as an almost immediate reality. She looks at his teeth and thinks of his skeleton, imagines him in his coffin. Her own future loneliness appalls her: "And then he will die. He will die before me. . . . I'll be alone beside his corpse." The idea of death gnaws away at her:

It's a day just like other days and the sky is outwardly blue. But
what a desert! Everything is silent. It's only the silence in my
head. There's no more love in me for anyone or anything.
What do distant galaxies and millions of men who will never
know me matter to me? I only have my own life and only it
matters, and now it doesn't matter any more, that's the point.
I don't see anything more to do on this earth. As for my
profession, what a joke! How could a person in my state have
the nerve to try to prevent a woman from weeping or help a
man sleep better?" (LM, p. 576)

Nadine, Robert, Lewis, none of them really need her any
more. She is useless. A faint flicker of memory of past
happiness and the charm of life assails her, but has no
effect. Memory of past happiness is only a goad to despair
because the past is irrevocable. This capitulation to despair is terribly distressing and seems to have been
precipitated by the now dead love affair, but the sweep-
ing rejection of life itself as a value because everything
passes away, and the insistent dwelling on death are the
expression of a permanent emotional tendency. Fortunately Anne resists the temptation of "easeful death",
for, as Simone de Beauvoir explains, suicide would have
been alien to her character.

In her exegesis of *Les Mandarins* Simone de Beauvoir
maintains that the novel is not a "roman à thèse"; there
is no didactic intent. She does say though that Anne
represents the philosophical idea of "being, the absolute
and death," which is opposed to that of the men who
choose action, limit, and life. However, she does regard
suicide as incompatible with Anne's temperament. She
explains Anne's choice:

Lastly, Anne does not kill herself; I didn't want to repeat the
error I made in *L'Invitée* of having my heroine's actions motivated by purely metaphysical reasons; Anne does not really

have the suicide's temperament, but still her final acceptance of the drab daily round is more like a defeat than a victory. In a story I wrote at eighteen, the heroine, on the last page, slowly descends the staircase which leads from her bedroom to the living room: she is going to find the others, and submit to their conventions and their lies thus betraying the "real life" she had caught a glimpse of in her solitude. It's not accidental that Anne, leaving her bedroom to join Dubreuilh descends a staircase; she too is betraying something. [LFDC, p. 290]

All this is very curious because it is difficult to see what Anne betrays when she consents to live, but Simone de Beauvoir seems to regard fierce intransigence and revolt against the paltriness of life as a heroic virtue and thus suicide becomes an admirable act. Unfortunately the quality of Anne's despair is so permeated with unjustified self-pity unwarranted by external events that the courageous heroism of this would-be suicide escapes the reader. It is pitiful rather than heroic. Simone de Beauvoir's comparison with a story written at eighteen is perhaps significant as it suggests the adolescent component of this kind of revolt against life.

At any rate Anne's suicide attempt illustrates her weakness which stems from complexities of character rather than from her status as a woman.[7] Simone de Beauvoir says that she gave Anne these negative traits which suit her general "passivity" of character. (LFDC, p. 284) But the complex ramifications of what Simone de Beauvoir really means by "passivity" or dependence could never be unraveled, for there is some fundamental ambiguity at the core of this baffling concept. On the one hand, Anne's attempted suicide results from her passivity and weakness shown in her morbid feelings about death, etc.; on the other hand, these feelings are at the same time presumably her strength and virtue since they express a noble refusal of limitation, mediocrity, and compromise; which appears contradictory.

Simone de Beauvoir acknowledges that her ideas in *The Second Sex* have some relevance to the feminine characters of her novels. She concedes that none of them ever achieve the ideal of independent, authentic human beings envisaged by *The Second Sex*. All are to some degree "relative and secondary beings." She explains why, without fully explaining:

> I've been reproached for not having chosen to represent my sex with a single woman who achieves equality with men by assuming the same professional and political responsibilities; in this novel I avoided the exceptional; I described women, in general, as I saw them, as I still see them: not whole, at war with themselves. . . . Anne gets nearer than the others to achieving real freedom; she doesn't succeed all the same in finding fulfillment in her own pursuits or career. None of them can be considered really positive heroines from the feminist point of view. I agree with the critics on this point, but I don't repent having depicted women like this. [LFDC, p. 286]

Simone de Beauvoir's refusal of the positive heroine is perplexing but consistent with *The Second Sex*. She does not *see* women as positive characters so why should she invent them? There remains the puzzle of herself. If she is positive, why not Anne?

It is to be expected that imaginative creations, if they are successful, will transcend abstract formula and defy consistency and logic by reflecting life's intractable complexities. Yet Simone de Beauvoir avers that her theory influences her fiction. What is striking, though, is that the two principal characters modelled on Simone de Beauvoir herself, Francoise and Anne, defy many of the categories and formulations of *The Second Sex*. Most of the other feminine characters are much more assimilable to its major assumptions. Anne, for instance, is an "amoureuse", but not in the invidious sense that Simone de Beauvoir develops in *The Second Sex*. She experiences love in the perfectly mixed up way of all human beings, and her love affair, deftly and movingly evoked, is drawn from the experience of the author. In this respect she is not a "relative being" but simply a woman in love and as such touching, generous, sad, and exhilarating. What then is the source of her dependence and weakness which are certainly aspects of her behavior? The entire thesis of *The Second Sex* is thoroughly vitiated in the case of Anne because she *has* a profession, a rather exacting one at that; it would be practically impossible to be a psychiatrist in a half-hearted, frivolous way. She is not financially dependent on Robert or Lewis. Simone de Beauvoir holds that her predominant interest in her family and lack of force and ambition make her traditionally feminine, dependent, and unsure of herself. But why does she not find "fulfillment in her own projects" Isn't this a question of character which transcends consideration of her feminine condition? Certainly on the surface Anne has all the attributes of resourceful independence; to be a psychiatrist *and* a wife and mother is rather an impressive feat. Yet at the end she is swept away by insufficiency, purposelessness and despair. Nothing sustains her; she is the antithesis of the brave Héloïse; she cries, "My profession, what a joke!" At this moment she displays the same kind of weakness Simone de Beauvoir remorselessly dissects in *The Second Sex,* that of the middle-aged woman, bereft of love, who cannot find joy or purpose in life, so barren and limited have been her horizons. Though Anne does not resemble this pitiable woman, for her life has been rarely rich and diverse, her defeat is identical.

She finds life a desert, "in ashes," and contemplates suicide. It is unjust and distorting to make these comparisons between fictional characters and pale abstract entities. But in this case it unearths what seems to be certain inconsistencies in Simone de Beauvoir's views about woman. What is one to make of the guilty "amoureuse" whose mistakenly limited way of life brings her to this desolate point of no return, while Anne, who has indeed been independent, contemplates suicide and regards the rest of her existence as a dreary "cell," no better than a death sentence? And then Simone de Beauvoir sees Anne's return to the world of the living and hope because people need her as a kind of defeat. It makes one's head swim. Despair is despair, but apparently it depends on who submits to it, and the appropriate philosophical nihilism evidently transforms ordinary despair in the face of griefs common to everyone into heroic courage.

Anne is a successful figure, complex and moving, who reflects much of Simone de Beauvoir's temperament as revealed in the autobiography. But her generous and outgoing qualities, including her attachment to her husband and daughter and her ardor and devotion to her lover are part of her strength, not indications of weakness and dependency. Strong feelings, disinterested affection and capacity for deep emotional attachments are a sign of vigor and force in anyone, man or woman. Anne's weakness seems to stem from some obscure part of her nature which is timid and self-effacing so that for some incomprehensible reason her profession does not absorb her fully. Is it because she is only a psychiatrist and not a writer like the brilliant male intellectuals in her circle? Impossible to tell. Her real weakness is a morbid preoccupation with nothingness and death, and it is this which wafts her to near self-destruction. She also lacks a certain inner conviction about her own worth and depends too much on what others feel about her. Thus the end of love which is a natural disaster assumes catastrophic proportions since without it she is nothing. Paradoxically one might say she is not sufficiently "philosophical" in the popular sense of that word.

The concluding chapter of Simone de Beauvoir's autobiography contains a celebrated passage in which the author plangently expresses her feelings about life at the age of fifty-four. It is a devastating document and to read it as the conclusion of this history of a stupendously energetic and gifted woman puts one in a state of near shock. This "cri du coeur," which is a protest against life itself and a refusal to accept with some kind of equanimity the cruel limitations of human existence, cuts into one's very marrow. What Simone de Beauvoir writes here is a striking echo of the words uttered by Anne as she contemplates suicide, except that here it is more painfully explicit, and since these are the words of a living woman they inspire pity and terror. Perhaps the key to this outburst is contained in Simone de Beauvoir's lifelong devotion to the absolute: "I had hardly any more desire to explore this earth emptied of its wonders; one expects nothing if one doesn't expect everything." (LFDC, p. 683) She is obsessed with old age, bodily decrepitude and death, and the horrors of her present life in no way make death appear a benign release—it hovers oppressively over her like an incubus. She awakens in the morning to the unbelievable reality of being fifty-four years old and this daily confrontation is a nightmare. She looks in the mirror and the description she gives of what she feels about her own face is harrowing. She is Anne magnified fifty times:

At the age of forty I thought, 'Old age lies in wait for me at the bottom of my mirror; it's inevitable; it will take hold of me.' Now it has. I pause, aghast, before this incredible object which functions as my face. I understand why Castiglione broke all the mirrors around him. I detest my own reflection; above my eyes is a kind of horrid cap and below them little pockets, my face is too full and has that sad look around the mouth which wrinkles cause. Perhaps the people who encounter me simply see a fifty-year-old woman who is neither beautiful nor ugly—she is only a woman of that age. But I see my former face which has been damaged beyond repair by the pox of age for which there is no cure.

Old age also afflicts my feelings. The nearness of my end and the inevitability of decay discourage my ardor for revolt; and happiness fades too. Death is no longer a brutal adventure in the dim future; it haunts my sleep.

Yes, the moment has arrived when I must say: never again —never again a man. . . . The only thing which can happen to me now is some misfortune. Either I will see Sartre die, or I will die before him. It is unbearably sad to imagine not being present to console the loved person for the pain you've inflicted by leaving him; it's equally desolate to envisage his death and his silence before your own. Nevertheless I detest as much as ever the thought of annihilation. [LFDC, p. 685]

Her past, her experience which any reader would find prodigious, her travels, her writing, her life—what do they mean to her now? She continues:

All those things I've written about and others about which I've said nothing—nothing of all that will remain. If at least my thought had given birth to——what? a hill? a rocket? But no. Nothing has taken place. I see again that hedgerow of hazel bushes softly jostled by the wind and all the promises which bewitched my heart when I gazed upon the splendors beckoning me on—a whole life ahead to live. The promises have been kept. Nevertheless, as I look back, wondering, on the credulous adolescent that I was, I am astonished when I realize how thoroughly I have been cheated. [LFDC, p. 686]

What can one say to such a shattering avowal? One might speak of the bankruptcy of Simone de Beauvoir's philosophy and so forth, but let us consider this simply in connection with Anne and *The Second Sex*. Like Anne, whom, however, Simone de Beauvoir intended as a dependent, not fully emancipated woman, Simone de Beauvoir succumbs to despair and the sense of the vanity of all things at the age of fifty-four, although she is in perfect health and has followed her own precepts. She has had a passionate commitment to ideas, to life, to her own work, to independence. And even according to the autobiography to "happiness." Only the ultimate mystery of individual temperament can explain this astonishing renouncement of life's value. Certainly such proclivities have been present in the writings of Simone de Beauvoir and in Anne, both of whom share the same morbid streak and who even exalt it and regard it as somehow exemplary. All the same, an ordinary reader of *The Second Sex*, a sad and discouraged "relative being" who finds bracing comfort and wisdom in Simone de Beauvoir's precepts will be sorely disappointed. The somber and desolate conclusion of *La Force des Choses* is certainly in one sense a betrayal of *The Second Sex*. If all Simone de Beauvoir's confident rationalism and theories about woman's liberation will not sustain her who has fully exemplified them, one might well ask—"à quoi bon?" However, this funereal mood certainly transcends sex and shows that character, temperament, strength or weakness, and personal philosophy are rooted in individual psychology so that the "situation" as a woman, enslaved or emancipated, cannot ultimately account for all reactions to the terrors of the human condition.

One could add, perhaps a bit uncharitably, that Simone de Beauvoir like Anne does in some sense share the traditional feminine attitudes she deplores in *The Second Sex,* since she puts so much value on her appearance. The sadness of getting old has a peculiar stygian horror for her as though all of her value as a human being disappeared with changes in her face. Perhaps it takes an exceptionally strong sense of the self to combat this natural feeling. No one can condemn such human and perhaps universal despair, but all the same this particular fixation is so feminine! Woman is "the erotic object" and the reflection of man's desire for her: this is the old refrain of *The Second Sex.* Its formulas, alas, cannot apparently extirpate the heavy weight of an ingrained cultural tradition and feminine psychology, nor alleviate the tragic limitations of human life.

NOTES

1. It is hard to take seriously, for instance, Simone de Beauvoir's introduction of Mme. de Warens and Léa who "play the virile and dominating role" as a genuine alternative to "the majority of cases where the woman only knows herself as the other." Simone de Beauvoir's insistence on the horror of dependence in women entails a corresponding exaggerated admiration for domination and virile strength. It is equality between the sexes and not domination by the woman that feminists have always sought. Feminists do not simply wish to reverse roles (as if they could!), but to eliminate role stereotypes and also *domination* of all kinds. *Human* liberation is the goal, not male subjection.

2. "Just as the men are all alike, so the women are various and individual, at once realistic and romantic. Women like these are not found in real life but only in the peculiar universe of Simone de Beauvoir. *L'Invitée* opens the doors to this universe, and Anne Dubreuilh is the sister of Françoise Miguel, as Nadine is another less odious version of the odious Xavière. In any case, whatever the character, from the moment a woman enters the scene and from the moment that love is involved everything gets stronger and brighter." Dominique Aury, "Personne ne triche," *La Nouvelle Revue Française,* 2e année, no. 24 (Dec. 1954), pp. 1080–85.

3. Simone de Beauvoir acknowledges that she endowed Anne with her

own negative obsessions with death, with nothingness and the absurdity of life. (LFDC, p. 288)

4. Aury, p. 1036.

5. Simone de Beauvoir is sometimes so resolutely sanguine (when she's not being apocalyptically gloomy) that woman's traditional suffering and woes can be somehow if not avoided at least transcended by sensible and energetic action. Thus she gives the following cheery picture of Héloise: "The failure of absolute love is a fruitful lesson only if the woman is capable of taking herself in hand again; separated from Abelard, Heloise was not wrecked, because she built herself an independent existence in the governing of an abbey." (TSS, II, p. 627) It's pleasant to think that Héloise did not succumb to despair and bravely constructed a useful life for herself; nevertheless the love of Abelard and Héloise obdurately resists such optimist interpretations as being only "a fruitful test" toward Héloise's future success as the competent directress of an abbey. It persists stubbornly in our imagination as one of history's tragic love affairs. No conceivable reform of woman's condition could ever cancel out the fact that love itself entails the tragedy of its loss.

6. Algren's own ideas about "contingent" love are interesting. "Anybody who can experience love contingently has a mind that has recently snapped. How can love be *contingent?* Contingent upon *what?* The woman is speaking as if the capacity to sustain Man's basic relationship—the physical love of man and woman—were a mutilation; while freedom consists of "maintaining through all deviations a certain fidelity!" What she means, of course, when stripped of its philosophical jargon, is that she and Sartre created a facade of petit-bourgeois respectability behind which she could continue to search for her own femininity. What Sartre had in mind when *he* left town I'm sure I don't know. . . ." Nelson Algren, "The Question of Simone de Beauvoir," *Harper's* (May 1965), p. 136.

7. "I have not," writes Mary Ellmann, "heard of women who have killed themselves simply and entirely because they are women." Margot Henthoff, "The Curse," review of *Thinking about Women*, by Mary Ellmann, *New York Review of Books* (16 Jan., 1969), p. 3.

4

Woman's Curse

THE CENTRAL THEME OF *LE DEUXIÈME SEXE* REFLECTED IN THE FEMININE CHARACTERS OF SIMONE DE BEAUVOIR'S NOVELS

At the beginning of *The Second Sex* Simone de Beauvoir denounces with admirable verve the peculiar and unflattering conception man has entertained about woman throughout the ages. She unmasks the characteristic bad faith with which a dominant group attributes the effects of its own oppression to the natural proclivities of its victims. Being herself a woman, she rightly feels more qualified to explore the subtle nuances of woman's condition and the tone she adopts has a fine militant ring:

> We shall not, then, permit ourselves to be intimidated by the number and violence of the attacks launched against women, nor to be entrapped by the self-seeking eulogies bestowed on the "true woman," nor to profit by the enthusiasm for woman's destiny manifested by men who would not for the world have any part of it. [TSS, I, p. xxvi]

In spite of her resolute feminism and trenchant analysis of how male-dominated culture influences in a negative way all of our thinking about women, she herself shares to some degree the misogyny she is attacking. She says: "Yes, women on the whole are today inferior to men;

that is to say, their situation opens up fewer possibilities."
(TSS, I, pp. xxiii–xxiv) Her constant theoretical insistence that none of woman's weaknesses and unattractive qualities are really her own fault but result from her situation mitigates the harshness of the indictment, but the fact remains that the work more often speaks with the voice of a judge than with that of an advocate.

In *La Force de L'Age,* Simone de Beauvoir disarmingly acknowledges her youthful propensity toward stern moralizing, a tendency which does not seem to have been mellowed by the years as it colors the emotive atmosphere of *Le Deuxième Sexe* and the autobiography. She writes:

> I agreed with Sartre on the importance of the individual person; but I was no less eager than he was to take people apart, recompose them and remodel their portraits; however, I wasn't much given to impartial observation. . . . I preferred judging them to understanding them. This moralism had strong and ancient roots in my character. The superiority my family plumed itself on had encouraged my arrogance; later solitude had helped to foster my somewhat aggressive pride. Circumstances also favored my penchant for sternness. Like all groups of young people, our little clan of friends would arrogantly divide the world up between two categories—the good and the bad; from the moment I joined the group I too would be merciless about everyone who didn't live up perfectly to our lofty standards; I was even more sectarian than Sartre or Pagniez; even if they executed their victims with ferocity, they did at least try to account for their victims' behavior. They would laugh amiably at what they called my "lack of psychology." [LFDL'A, p. 144]

Thus when Simone de Beauvoir attempts to show how the situation imposed upon woman has adversely affected both her capacity for happiness and her moral character, her examples are so extremely negative that her book appears to have been written by a misogynist. The following examples are picked at random and typify Simone de Beauvoir's normal tone of voice: "Most women simultaneously demand and detest their feminine condition; they live it through in a state of resentment. The disgust they have for their sex might well lead them to give their daughters a man's education, but they are rarely large-minded enough. Vexed at having produced a woman, the mother greets her with this ambiguous curse: 'You shall be a woman.'" (TSS, II, p. 489) The faults that women are supposed to have they do in fact have: "Many of the faults that are attributed to women: mediocrity, pettiness, timidity, meanness, laziness, frivolity and servility simply express the fact that their horizons are severely limited." (TSS, II, p. 568) Simone de Beauvoir does not protest against the patent injustice and absurdity of attributing these faults to one sex. She accepts the charge as valid, even though forced by circumstances. As though "mediocrity," "pettiness," "timidity," "laziness," et al. were uniquely feminine preogatives! Then there is the following on woman's "animality":

> If she seems to man so "physical" a creature, it is because her situation leads her to attach extreme importance to her animal nature. The call of the flesh is no louder in her than in the male, but she catches its least murmurs and amplifies them. Sexual pleasure, like rending pain, represents the stunning triumph of the immediate; in the violence of the instant, the future and the universe are denied; what lies outside the carnal flame is nothing; for the brief moment of this apotheosis, woman is no longer mutilated and frustrated. But, once again, she values these triumphs of immanence only because immanence is her lot. [TSS, II, p. 568]

Despite the mitigating excuses (this is all she is given to do!) and the florid rhetoric, there is not much to distinguish such an opinion of woman from the thundering condemnation of old testament prophets—woman is "flesh," the source of sin and woe. It does seem unsporting to talk disparagingly about woman's "animality" while devoting almost an entire volume to the minutiae of woman's erotic life.[1] It appears that Simone de Beauvoir's existentialist bias makes her regard the natural and the physical as somehow demeaning since they involve "immanence." But she also takes the opposite view. Many women are frigid, puritanical, horrified of the physical side of life. This hostility to experience extends to everything so that all natural joy is extinguished as they seek to preserve their figures, their complexions and their clean houses at the price of spoiling everyone else's fun. They are puritanical kill-joys. (TSS, II, p. 505) Woman's basic dependence on men and the necessity of attracting and holding him by means of a beautiful exterior make her false and theatrical; the outer husk is all. That is to say, woman is the insincere sex just as all the ancient misogynist clichés maintain. Furthermore, women are catty and untrustworthy because they compete with other women for men; true friendship between women is rare and undermined by female jealousy. Women "friends" usually spend much of their time concocting plots against men, revenging themselves on them, belittling men, but the pathetic reality of all this malevolence is that the male wins since *he* is the center of all their attention. Etc., etc., etc., etc. This melancholy litany of woman's unattractive qualities continues unabated with the rare intervention of a bright exception, instantly crushed by another negative example or diminished by qualifications. It is not a pretty picture. *The Second Sex* is a long and dolorous lamentation about woman's woes but also a diatribe against the female sex.

Though woman is also pictured as a *pathetic* creature and thus worthy of our sympathy, her behavior and her character are not inspiring. It seems fair to conclude that Simone de Beauvoir shares in part the anti-feminism she condemns. Her "feminist" opinions acquire ironic flavor with hindsight.

This deeply-seated attitude expresses itself emphatically though in a subtler way in the novels where Simone de Beauvoir has created a splendid array of feminine characters who might be said to illustrate the melancholy thesis of *The Second Sex.* In this respect, there is a rigorous consistency in Simone'de Beauvoir's work. Her feminine characters are indeed incarnations of *The Second Sex,* sad and divided creatures, but they are for the most part animated, startling and humanly believable and thus more convincing than the abstract, exaggerated and rather chilling stereotypes of *Le Deuxième Sexe.* Although the "woman question" is never an open issue, they embody vividly in themselves most feminine weaknesses, conflicts, and tragic limitations. No wonder, since Simone de Beauvoir confesses: "I described women in general as I saw them and as I still see them: divided." Two basic premises: woman is "divided" and a "sad" creature, form the double fundamental flaw of character of most fictional heroines of Simone de Beauvoir. However, their compound failings assume many forms. Six particularly flawed examples will serve to show how Simone de Beauvoir's inspiration plays variations on the same theme.

One of the saddest figures is Paule, the mistress of Henri Perron in *Les Mandarins.* She is a fictional composite of several of the unsalubrious traits that *The Second Sex* exposes with such unsparing exactitude. She is an "amoureuse" of the most unhealthy persuasion; she is a narcissist; she lives "through" another in a parasitical and frightening way; she is riddled with bad faith and self-deception; she is woefully dependent on a man and she doesn't earn her own living. She is not even a mother. Eventually she succumbs to outright paranoia and, though superficially cured afterward, her whole life is revealed as a tragic waste. She is not very admirable; her self-reinforcing narrow egotism, tyrannical and megalomaniacal behavior are sometimes downright atrocious, but in the main she arouses pity rather than contempt. If she has indeed created much of her own misery, it seems inevitable; she is a helpless victim of her character and destiny and it is not irrelevant that it is peculiarly a woman's destiny. Her punishment is cruelly disproportionate to her crime.

Paule, a great beauty and a singer of some renown in her youth, has lived as Henri's mistress for ten years. Their love affair had been a "grand amour." But unfortunately she has given her life to it, while Henri is absorbed in his writing, politics, and the fascinating world outside. Hemmed in and oppressed by the smothering totality of Paule's devotion, he tires of her and wishes to break off. This is not easy, however, since Paule has transformed herself into a sacrificial victim. Henri's rueful and frustrated attempts to detach himself finally from this "preying mantis" consume much of Paule's history in the novel. Simone de Beauvoir extracts every painful ounce from this degenerating relationship: Paule's abnegation, abject humility, acceptance of the merest crumbs and massive self-deception are pitiful in the extreme, while conversely her abnormal obsession with Henri and the way in which her "generosity" becomes suffocating domination are blood-curdling.

The uncomfortable situation is immediately apparent. Paule's behavior demonstrates the formidable obstacles

Henri faces. She hovers about him, waiting on him, offering him dainty little pieces of toast at breakfast, setting flowers on the table and humming gaily, all in her attempt to be the perfect loving handmaiden because, after all, Henri is her life. She is never spontaneous and natural; all her actions have a stagey quality about them. She sits looking at magazine pictures which show Henri, famous writer, during a trip to Portugal with Nadine.[2] The conversation leads up to her main theme which is that only she can preserve Henri's grandeur; she loathes sordid compromise and expects heroism from him. Paule leafs through a photo album admiring Henri's baby pictures and making comments which make Henri writhe because they are so possessive and so subtly aimed at veiled criticism of Henri. Henri thinks: "Paule hadn't contradicted herself exactly but her attitude infuriated Henri: she wanted him to be famous and yet she pretended to scorn fame and she insisted upon seeing herself just exactly like Henri's romantic conception of her at the beginning—haughty and sublime; meanwhile in fact she inhabited this dull world like everyone else. 'And it's not a very amusing life for her,' he thought, with sudden pity, 'It's quite natural for her to need some kind of compensation.' " (LM, p. 118) The crux of Paule's tragic situation is indicated at this moment: her obsession with Henri, her dangerous vicarious way of living and her lofty moral principles which remain idle abstractions since they are always invoked in behalf of Henri, not herself. Henri is trapped by his natural sympathy and sense of honor but ultimately he must escape. He sensibly tries to interest her in *doing* something and suggests that she take up her singing again. Their conversation starts with an account of Paule's day which could serve as a tract for *The Second Sex:*

—'What are you going to do today?' he asked affectionately.
—'Nothing special.'
—'But what?'
—She thought it over. 'Well, I'm going to telephone a dress-maker to ask her to look at that beautiful cloth you brought me.'
—'And after that?'
—'Oh, I always have things to do,' she said gaily.
—'That means you don't really do a thing,' Henri said. He looked at Paule sternly. 'I've thought a lot about you this month. I think it's criminal that you spend your days vegetating between these four walls.
—'You call this vegetating!' responded Paule. She smiled sweetly and as in the old days all the wisdom of the world appeared in her smile. 'When you love, you don't vegetate.'
—'But love isn't an occupation.' She interrupted him hotly: 'I beg your pardon, it's *my* occupation.' [LM, p. 118]

For a woman who has lived with a man ten years this is a frightening avowal, and borders on the pathological; Paule does in fact harbor incipient madness. She is "l'amoureuse à outrance." Henri enthusiastically conjures up visions of a new career, recalls Paule's earlier triumphs and is bursting with schemes to find songs, contacts, etc. He is up against a stone wall. Paule indignantly rejects his suggestions and erupts with revealing bitterness about the past, saying that years ago when she sacrificed an engagement in Brazil for him that meant the final renunciation of her career. Furthermore she says fame means nothing to her though she would find it impossible now to start a "second-rate career" at the age of thirty-seven. Henri is nonplussed and angry since her interpretation of the past is so false and unjust. He had never asked her to sacrifice anything—but he contains himself. Paule is an enigma. "He'd never know whether she really scorned success or whether she merely feared not attaining it." (LM, p 118) The fatal mistake of living for love is evident. Paule becomes super-sensitive to injury, excessively proud and haughty, while at the same time enjoying the insidious kind of noble martyrdom common to those masochistic females of *The Second Sex* who so delight in the pleasures of self-sacrifice and renunciation.

Paule obviously shares many of the traits common to the narcissist whom Simone de Beauvoir pictures as the woman who seeks to conceal her basic dependency by concentrating on a cult of the self which is a doomed enterprise since maniacal egoism can only rest on illusion and falsehood and stems from fundamental inauthenticity. Paule's narcissism is reflected in her obsession with Henri's "gloire", her idolatry of him as an artist, and her appalling delusion that somehow *she* is the fount from which all his creative energies flow. In *The Second Sex* Simone de Beauvoir displays a crowded gallery of these vampirish women. There is Georgette Leblanc, who wished to be for Maeterlinck "aliment et flamme," and the redoubtable Mabel Dodge whose frank admission about her desire to inspire D. H. Lawrence's work contains a lucid self-appraisal about the negative source of her impulse: "I wanted to win over his mind and to compel it to create certain things. I needed his soul, his will, his creative imagination and luminous vision. To make myself the master of these essential tools I had to dominate his strength. I had always sought to make other people create without attempting to do anything whatsoever myself. This way I felt I might somehow be compensated for my desperate feeling of having nothing at all to do." (TSS, II, p. 599)

Similarly, Paule plays the unwelcome role of Egeria to Henri but in such an extreme fashion that the egoism behind the beneficent concern is painfully transparent. Anne visits Paule and, aware of her increasing turmoil, also urges her to find some work to occupy her life. Paule receives her in an appropriately parasitical costume; she trails about the house in taffeta and high-heeled slippers; indolent, vain, untidy and self-indulgent. Anne gets nowhere with her advice since Paule must devote all of her time to *Henri's* work! Under the guise of noble altruism Paule betrays a monstrous, pathological egoism. She cunningly twists reality to conform with her own version of herself and the world. In a frenzy of self-justification and pathetic deluded grandeur she proclaims haughtily: "I don't pretend to be infallible, but you realize that it's I who have made Henri; I've created him just as he's created the characters in his books, and I know him in the same way as he knows them. He's in danger now of betraying his mission and I'm the one who must lead him back to it. And that's why I couldn't dream of looking after myself and my own puny interests." (LM, p. 177) She is of course deranged, but this paroxysm of bad faith is characteristic of narcissistic women according to Simone de Beauvoir and Paule can be seen as a case history of the genre. The narcissist, enveloped in her own phantom world where she must be queen and superior being, is blind to the pathetic and ridiculous figure she actually cuts.

Paule becomes more and more divorced from reality until finally she exhibits the symptoms of real erotomania in which she converts all the indubitable evidence of Henri's indifference into certain proof of his love for her. Exasperated beyond endurance by Paule's imperious nagging about his work, he first refuses to let her see his most recent novel, because he has invented a most unflattering female character based on her, but finally gives her the manuscript, knowing it will wound her but hoping it will also shake her incredible illusions. Paule's reaction is totally unforseen; she is gay and admiring and calls it a masterpiece—another one of her theatrical performances; but from this point on she disintegrates rapidly, displaying signs of pathological derangement. When Henri openly demands that she face up to the end of their love and offers her friendship, she answers with a secret smile: she knows he really loves *her*. She is clearly unhinged. Paule's breakdown resembles in remarkable detail Simone de Beauvoir's scary portrait of the narcissist in *The Second Sex* whose fanatical devotion to protecting her own self image at the center of her own private universe ends finally in total disintegration and disastrous mental alienation. Narcissism is in short a sterile raison d'être and can lead to madness. Paule's condition is pathological, but Simone de Beauvoir sees her primarily as a victim of her "situation" as a woman rather than of mental illness. The narcissist may end up a mental case, but the roots of her disease lie in her "feminine" choice of a mode of life. According to Simone de Beauvoir this is a characteristic feminine life style which woman's unhappy situation fosters. In speaking of *Les Mandarins* she says: "Paule clings to traditional feminine values: they are not adequate for her, and she is torn apart to the point of madness." (LFDC, p. 286)

In *Le Sang des Autres*, Simone de Beauvoir's novel about the Resistance with heavy existentialist overtones, the heroine Hélène is much more enterprising and energetic than Paule, less passive and unhealthily wound up in herself. She dies heroically, thus achieving "transcendence" in a traditionally masculine way. Nevertheless Hélène represents all too clearly the feminine failings and evasions that *The Second Sex* flails so relentlessly. Her character and temperament, typically feminine, compel her to behave selfishly even in an extreme situation when others rise to unexpected heroism. For Hélène too is an "amoureuse." Her deification of love and her belief in the priority of private happiness make her react in a typically feminine way when the placidity of her own life is challenged by the moral ambiguities of war and Resistance.

Hélène is a petite bourgeoise who works as a clothes designer. Initially engaged to Paul, an amiable, earnest, and plodding young man of the working class, she meets Jean Blomart—the hero of the novel—whose single-minded ardor and mysterious sense of mission capture her romantic imagination. She pursues him shamelessly with a fury of self-abasement. She only succeeds in capturing him through pity when Jean is forced to witness a grisly abortion she undergoes—the result of a wild drunken episode after Hélène felt violently thwarted by Jean's indifference. Jean consents to be Hélène's lover and then her husband, but he does this mainly through guilt and pity for her sufferings, which he has partly caused by simply *being* there. Though her life becomes then wrapped up in her love for Jean in the best "amoureuse" fashion, it remains a strangely one-sided and unreciprocal passion. It is indeed a blessing that Hélène cannot fathom Jean Blomart's self-doubt and torment and the real basis of his pallid affection for her.

At first, Hélène is rather captivating since she exudes gaiety and verve. She is capricious, willful and petulant and has her own kind of perverse charm. On a mad impulse she steals the bicycle of her concierge to join Paul at a restaurant where she is to meet Jean Blomart. Her wide-eyed fascination and covetousness as she contemplates the wonder of the resplendent bicycle is absurd in a woman her age but rather ingratiating in its naïve rapture. She is frivolous and avid for life and adventure in a childish way, but her candor and spontaneousness make her attractive. Her cultivation of an intensely romantic attitude about love is part of her irrational and emotional feminine nature, although, as Simone de Beauvoir is at pains to point out, her bourgeois origins have also something to do with this. An aphorism from *The Second Sex* holds that men like to encourage women's failings by loving them for their very faults and weaknesses: "If woman is not treacherous, frivolous, frightened and indolent, she loses her attractiveness." Hélène does not embody the worst of these; she is warm-hearted and generous and she *works*, but she exemplifies in many respects those light-weight qualities of "the eternal feminine" that Simone de Beauvoir always so soundly denounces.

Hélène is fond of Paul, but she is infuriated by his placid acceptance of love as a comfortable down-to-earth emotion without drama and scalding passions. He regards her romantic attitudes as typically bourgeois and joshes her affectionately about them. Hélène, bourgeois individualist to the core, scorns Paul's good-natured common sense because it devaluates her and makes life seem dull and ordinary. Simone de Beauvoir has in fact given Hélène some of her own youthful manias. Even as a child she was a passionate individualist and regarded herself as unique and rare. She detested the condescension of adults toward children because that minimized her own sense of splendid uniqueness: "The patronizing attitudes of adults often makes children seem to belong to a faceless race of beings who are totally undifferentiated; nothing irritated me more than that. At La Grillère one time when I was munching on some hazel nuts the spinster who was employed as Madeline's tutor declared pedantically: 'Children just adore hazel-nuts.' I made fun of her later to Poupette; I knew my tastes were not ordained by my age; I wasn't a child; I was *me.*" (MD'UJFR, p. 59) The intense individualism of the young Simone de Beauvoir is mixed with a tendency toward excess that has little patience with the docility and common sense of most people. She writes: "What separated me from the others was a certain violence which I only encountered in myself. I liked Pradelle a lot but he was so untormented. His calm detachment hurt me." (MD'UJFR, p. 248) Simone de Beauvoir endowed Hélène with her own fiery nature which explains Hélène's considerable attractiveness. But unlike the author she is frivolous to a fault and her ardor for life and excitement does not take constructive or self-transcendent directions. Jean Blomart, wrapped up in his syndicalism, is not at all in the mood to be seduced by this demanding and impetuous girl but he is not insensible to her considerable charm. Hélène writes him letters and pursues him brazenly. Jean finally consents to a meeting. He talks about the strikes in France and everything that interests him intensely. Hélène's frivolity annoys him. His strikes bore her. Despite Hélène's self-absorption and lack of seriousness, Jean is attracted by her intensity. She is immune to his polite rebuffs and disarmingly candid. What attracts him is her sincerity. Hélène has immense vitality which childish selfishness can't spoil. She has the generous spirit of the "vraie amoureuse" rather than the calculating self-regard of the narcissist. Jean Blomart cannot really resist her and he is indulgent with her failings. They finally marry and Hélène is happy. But when the war breaks out, her foolish addiction to comfort and private happiness cause her to connive to get Jean transferred to a soft job behind the lines. Aghast and angry at this selfishness, obtuseness, and incomprehension of what really matters to him, he breaks with her. A previous conversation between Jean and Hélène show the tenacity with which she vainly attempts to save her own cozy world while everything goes up in flames around her:

> Helene bit her lips. 'They'll win the war all right without you,' she said.
> 'Listen, Hélène, can you really imagine that I could hide cowering in a little quiet corner while my friends let themselves be killed?'
> —'I don't give a damn about the others,' said Hélène despairingly. 'I don't owe anything to anybody.' She burst out sobbing. 'I'll kill myself if you die and I don't want to die.'
> —'Can't you try, just once, to think about somebody besides yourself?' Jean said.

According to *The Second Sex* this kind of complacent cowardice and egocentricity are characteristically feminine; women are traditionally conservative and reactionary in politics for this reason:

> as woman takes no part in history, she fails to understand its necessities; she is suspiciously doubtful of the future and wants to arrest the flow of time. . . . They [women] seek to compensate for their inactivity by the intensity of the sentiments they exhibit. With victory won, they rush like hyenas upon the fallen foe; in defeat, they bitterly reject any efforts at conciliation. Their ideas being merely attitudes, they support quite unconcernedly the most outdated causes. . . . In women's eyes, might makes right because the rights she recognizes in men depend upon their power. Hence it is, that when a society breaks down, women are the first to throw themselves at the feet of the conqueror. On the whole they accept what is. [TSS, II, pp. 565–66]

Simone de Beauvoir's habitual unflattering ferocity in regard to the female sex is in full flower here. Fortunately Hélène does not conform entirely to these harsh prescriptions. After Jean breaks with her, she mournfully resumes her life in Paris where her natural generosity and imaginative sympathy are finally shaken into wrath and indignation by the horrors inflicted on her friends and the people around her. She returns to Jean who now leads a group in the Resistance and she dies heroically. Nonetheless Hélène's failings are typically feminine ones and mar her character. In fact there is almost too much demonstration of clear-cut moral truths in this novel and Simone de Beauvoir herself regards *Le Sang des Autres* as being too didactic. She shows implacable severity toward this novel when she says about it: "I wanted to believe that I could speak to my public directly, whereas actually my more pathetic and moralistic side had imperiously taken over; . . . You can't have original ideas either in salons or in novels. The novel with a message not only does not prove anything, but its ideas are inferior ones." (LFDL'A, p. 629) Thus Hélène's return to Jean and to a moral reawakening has something too neat and pat about it; the reader is unpleasantly aware of the author's manipulation of her characters to suit a didactic purpose. Hélène is drawn as frivolously feminine but when she commits herself to work for the Resistance she is redeemed through action. In a few lines of conversation between Jean and Hélène, (LSDA, p. 220) the author states that transcendence can save one, that a woman confined in her own narrow circle can escape selfish egoism by having "something to do", that Hélène's love for Jean can only be vindicated if she shares his ideals which are more important than either of them, that dying for a cause can give life a meaning, and that Hélène's character is fundamentally generous so that this decision is really predictable and consistent with her past action. It is too neat and schematic. However, Hélène, as Simone de Beauvoir herself admits, is the most believable and multidimensional character in the novel, more successful than the rest who lack "density", because she has some of the author's own qualities. Hélène is the only one of Simone de Beauvoir's feminine characters to engage in heroic masculine action. Like Françoise and Anne, who also benefit from Simone de Beauvoir's autobiographical closeness, she is flawed and weak but ultimately admirable. All the same, she too is afflicted with notable defects and her moral transformation owes far too much to the author's didactic intention.

Although women artists have to some extent surmounted the handicap of being feminine, Simone de Beauvoir finds that femininity gravely impedes artistic endeavor. She connects the artistic impulse in women with narcissism and exposes the half-hearted dilettantism, self-adulation, and spurious sensibility that propels them to write, paint, or be actresses without any real sense of vocation or total commitment to the agonizing *work* that art demands. Woman's natural laziness and vanity erode her artistic efforts:

> Even if she begins fairly early, she seldom envisages art as serious work; accustomed to idleness, having never felt in her mode of life the austere necessity of discipline, she will not be capable of sustained and persistent effort, she will never succeed in gaining a solid technique. She is repelled by the thankless, solitary gropings of work that never sees the light of day, that must be destroyed and done over a hundred times; and as from infancy she has been taught trickery when learning to please, she hopes to "get by" through the use of a few stratagems. Marie Bashkirtsev admits precisely that: "Yes, I never

take the trouble to paint. I watched myself today. I *cheat."*
[TSS, II, p. 663]

This is quite acute and pins down with beautiful precision
a certain kind of "artistic" woman, but it also demonstrates Simone de Beauvoir's constant bias against
women. It is hard to accept the dictum that in being
taught to please women are taught to cheat. She goes on
to say that women tend to regard their art as merely
decorative extensions of themselves. Their fundamental
purpose is narcissistic and their art exists to reflect *them.*
"Moreover, it is her own self that is the principal—sometimes the unique subject of interest to her: Mme. Vigée-
Lebrun never wearied of putting her smiling maternity
on her canvases." (TSS, II, p. 665) In her novels, Simone
de Beauvoir has created some female would-be artists, all
of whom are fatally afflicted with bad faith and mediocrity. They are suffering, divided beings who seek to justify themselves through art, but their artistic impulses
spring primarily from a quest for "gloire" and approval.
They are all neurotic in the extreme, but their neurosis
does not bear noble fruit as in the case of the grand,
suffering male artists. They all exemplify in some measure Simone de Beauvoir's strictures about women artists
who are too inclined to be complacent, indolent, and
insincere.

The most successful woman artist is Elisabeth, the pathetic but terrifying sister of Pierre Labrousse in *L'Invitée.*
She is tormented by a sense of her own unworthiness and
emptiness and is obsessed with the impression she makes
on others. *L'Invitée* predates *The Second Sex* by six years,
but the character of Elisabeth is an apt precursor of that
work. She fatally lacks strong conviction and consequently is consumed with all the negative emotions: re-

sentment, envy, rancor, hate, self-pity, vengefulness, cynicism and, above all, falsity and insincerity. She constantly fabricates a self and attitudes in a desperate attempt to be *somebody,* but she betrays her basic hollowness in every word and gesture.

More than any other character, Elisabeth best personifies the dictum of *The Second Sex* that woman is an *object.* Woman's servitude to looking elegant and beautiful is real, since her life literally depends upon how she looks. Her clothes, coiffure, and make-up represent not just aesthetic satisfaction and pleasure in looking nice but are the real lures necessary for the serious business of survival. Elisabeth is an eager adherent of this depressing doctrine. She appears to believe that her life literally depends on her appearance. She ruminates that if only she had more money she might win this horrible battle of the beautiful exterior. She spills a bottle of nail polish on her lovely manicure just before leaving for the theatre and weeps bitterly. Her thoughts show the pathetic machinations of a woman-object whose life is an unremitting struggle to present a charming surface to the world. She never questions the validity of this concept; she simply feels envy and resentment of parasitical women with enough money to soften the rigors of this unending battle.

Elisabeth is so lost that the outside world is threatening and strange to her, a veritable jungle. She mistrusts and suspects everyone, and all of her relations with other people are dictated by Machiavellian strategies of guile and subterfuge. She is constantly obsessed by what other people think of her, and of course she will never know. She must constantly observe herself and feverishly invent postures that create a favorable impression. "Had Claude already arrived? What was she going to say? She glanced quickly in the mirror, she didn't look too ravaged, but there wasn't enough time to think up how she should act." (*L'Invitée,* p. 83)

As one could expect, Elisabeth is also a case of the false "amoureuse". She is the mistress of a truly miserable specimen named Claude: a bad writer, extremely vain and superficial, avid for success, who is a male version of Elisabeth, riddled with bad faith, who values nothing but appearances. Elisabeth who has flashes of lucidity sees all this and even hates him; yet she abjectly clings to him because her empty life demands at least the illusion of being loved. To be admired and have a man in tow is essential. Elisabeth imagines life without Claude and can only conjure up a great vision of emptiness. This is ironic because the real emptiness is situated in the depths of Elisabeth's own being. She evokes quite well the feeling often generated in *The Second Sex* that life for women who depend on men is a perpetual battleground with fear of abandonment always looming in the future. Younger, more beautiful women are always waiting in the wings and so there is no haven of safety, no respite, but just a losing struggle which old age inevitably terminates. Of course Elisabeth and Claude are pitiful and contemptible but no more than the shadowy figures of *The Second Sex.* As Claude refuses to leave his wife, Elisabeth attempts to revive his love by grubby infidelities with "types," whereupon Claude instead of exploding with jealousy just takes up the bait and maintains that her example inspires him: "After all, he said, "That's a solution. I've often thought it was a pity that an artist should limit himself to one woman." (He already has two!) (*L'Invitée,* p. 98) Elisabeth realizes with horror what hopeless vistas she has opened up: "She pressed her handkerchief between her moist hands; now she recognized the danger and it was too late—there wasn't any way to retreat. She had only thought about Suzanne, but there were all the other women, young and beautiful women who would love Claude and would know how to win his love." (*L'Invitée*, p. 980)

Elisabeth's painting reflects the shallowness of her character; she paints because the idea of *being* an artist flatters her vanity, but actually painting with passion and tenacity is not in the least congenial to her. The horror is that she dimly realizes this. Simone de Beauvoir makes Elisabeth one of those unfortunates who actually have some insight into their own futility but are powerless to change. Note Elisabeth's reaction when showing her paintings to Pierre, Françoise and Xavière: "I'm having a new evolutionary stage," Elisabeth quipped with heavy irony. Her pictures: colors spread out on canvas so that they looked like pictures; she spent days painting to convince herself she was a painter, but it was still only a dismal pretense. She was going to show them her fake pictures and they would shower fake praise on her. They wouldn't know what she knew; in this respect they were the ones who were taken in." (*L'Invitée*, p. 270) In spite of this self-protective self-denigration and frequent flashes of piercing lucidity, Elisabeth is so profoundly given to rationalization that moments later she wistfully concludes that if she only had an audience she could do great things. All of her failings are ultimately blamed on other people, destiny, bad luck, etc. Simone de Beauvoir has perhaps tried to "demonstrate" a bit too much with Elisabeth, who at times almost borders on caricature, so monstrous are her rancorous resentments and her venimous spirit. Her malevolence is impressive, however. She is a classic example of the negative pronouncements of *The Second Sex* about the complacent attitudes and mistaken motivations that are responsible for much mediocre work that women artists produce. It is not so much lack of talent as fallacious and trivial purposes that impair so much feminine artistic effort. Simone de Beauvoir believes that sincerity, patience, energy, and a powerful will are as vital as talent or genius in artistic creation, and these qualities are what women often sadly lack.

Another similarly afflicted would-be artist is Denise in *Le Sang des Autres.* However, she shares the general weakness of this novel. As Simone de Beauvoir says, "What I find striking in this novel is to what degree my characters lack density: they are determined by moral attitudes whose concrete causes I didn't manage to convey." (LFDC, p. 625) Denise offers another almost too insistent example of an unhappy woman who has nothing to do and who attempts to write novels simply to satisfy her forlorn cravings for self-importance and to fill in the void she feels in herself. She had been a brilliant student but derives all her dreams of success and glory through the artistic triumphs of her husband Marcel. At first, after a show of his paintings she glows with rapture. But she is primarily interested in worldly success, and becomes disappointed when Marcel, an eccentric and somewhat demented artist who yearns for absolute perfection, renounces his painting for chess. His defection leaves her utterly disoriented and, to compensate it, she furiously plunges into various activities, political action, and then writing novels, for which she has no particular talent. She pours herself with wild energy into her projects but satisfaction and success always elude her. Hélène remarks about her: "Poor Denise! She's the one who wanted so desperately to have a genius in the house." (LSDA, p. 129) Since her husband Marcel is cruel, caustic, condescending, and indifferent, she certainly has objective grounds for her misery, but her inner lack of self-esteem gives every set-back pathetic dimensions. At dinner in a restaurant with Jean, Hélène, and Marcel, after having earlier received Jean's harsh verdict on her novel, Denise has a violent emotional outburst provoked in part by Marcel's cruel gibes. She strikes out at Jean, who tries to be kind and conciliating: "Yes, you don't give a damn about it," she said harshly. "You have your unions, Marcel has his chess, and Hélène has you. But me . . . she said with a suppressed sob, "Me, I have nothing." (LSDA, p. 138) Unfortunately Jean's forthright criticism of Denise's novel is all too applicable to *Le Sang des Autres:* "You explain too much," said Jean. "But you don't show anything. You tell what you have to about them (the characters), but you don't bring them to life—they're terribly abstract." (LSDA, p. 134) Denise might have strayed in unannounced from *The Second Sex* as she demonstrates so neatly Simone de Beauvoir's ideas about the emptiness of women with scarred psyches. The source of her malaise is not entirely clear, but one suspects that much of it springs from the malediction of being a woman. Jean reflects: "I looked at her with great sympathy. She had many fine qualities. She accepted poverty without complaint, she never reproached Marcel, she tried manfully to understand what she called her "complex". She was loyal, intelligent and brave. But some hidden defect marred all these good traits." (LSDA, p. 61) Even her "virtues" will not redeem her. She is another fatally flawed Beauvoirian woman whose feminine condition imposes too great a burden on her fragile spirit.

Another narcissist and artist is Régine in the unusual *Tous les Hommes Sont Mortels,* which is a historical fantasy with existentialist overtones. Régine fails to assume real life-size dimensions and remains even more shadowy and abstract than the hypothetical figures of *The Second Sex.* In a review of this novel, Joé Bousquet, who admires Simone de Beauvoir's gifts, puts his finger on the trouble: "Perhaps I should add, that it is paradoxically her good faith and integrity that prevent her from mastering certain literary problems. She is the victim of her moral gifts because she uses them for aesthetic purposes." He describes Régine and her maid, Annie: "Heartless females who have never learned how to smile. They only possess will and they try to invent feelings by imagining themselves the opposite of what they experience."[3] The redoutable Régine's unreality astonishes because though she is all violence and extremes, sound and fury do not necessarily generate flesh and blood. Régine is interesting because she is an extreme case of the ravening egotistical female, the insatiable narcissist, who, not content with universal adoration and worldly triumph, must attain the love of the immortal Fosca in order to be loved and admired throughout eternity. She is haunted by death and nothingness, and has an absolutist yearning to be everything; but her torments and wild ravings about "being" are impossible to accept at face value because she does not speak or act like a recognizable human being.

Régine is a successful actress, and driven by an implacable will, she thirsts for fame. All the same life has the taste of ashes and cinders in her mouth and she scorns and detests just about everyone. When she reveals her most sadistic, vengeful, and cynical feelings to her maid, Annie, she seems motivated by some nameless rage: "She loathed her coiffure and makeup; she detested the smiles she felt herself making and all the artful modulations of her voice. 'It's degrading,' she thought to herself angrily, and then she thought, 'Later, I'll have my revenge.' " (TLHSM, p. 30) One is at a loss to understand this smouldering fury. Apparently she aspires to acclaim but scorns the trappings and compromises that this entails. A real narcissist would enjoy the coiffure, the makeup, and all the rest. Régine cannot bear to contemplate anyone else's happiness; she is consumed with envy and spite; she treats people abominably; and then she haughtily proclaims her aristocratic disdain for mediocrity and pettiness. But she herself is not generous or magnanimous; in fact, quite the contrary. After a frightful scene with Annie she confesses to Fosca: "You've discovered that I'm wicked. It's true. I don't like to see other people happy and I'm glad to make them feel the power I have over them. Annie wouldn't get in my way; it's just for spite that I won't bring her along." (TLHSM, p. 65) Unfortunately Regine's "sincerity" does not add to her charm. And yet Fosca can say to her: "I see you. You are blonde, generous and ambitious, you have a horror of death." (TLHSM, p. 71) Yet Régine never exhibits the tiniest inkling of generosity and her fictional thinness arises from fundamental contradictions of this nature. How anyone who cannot tolerate other people's happiness could be generous is not clear. She is a kind of ogress—a grotesque manifestation of the extreme narcissist of *The Second Sex.* Régine never thinks of her lover, only of herself; Fosca's immortality constitutes his only attraction; with Fosca her triumph as Rosalind could last forever. "From the farthest limit of eternity he would watch me and Rosalind would become immortal." (TLHSM, p. 42)

Simone de Beauvoir's account of her plan for Régine explains as well as anything Régine's failure to materialize convincingly because, even in conception, she strains credulity and is made to serve too handily Simone de Beauvoir's thematic purpose. Régine is conceived as a "counterpoint to Fosca's drama": "I provided him with a woman avid for domination who was in revolt against all human limits: other's fame and her own death; when she meets Fosca she wants to live in his immortal soul; then finally she thinks she will become unique; just the opposite happens: she dissolves before his eyes; her condition and talents only disclose how ridiculous is her attempt to set herself above all other people since they all must die; terror-stricken, she watches her life disintegrate into a horrible farce; she goes mad." (LFDC, p. 78) Régine has remote affinities with other de Beauvoir heroines and the author herself (Paule, Anne, Denise, Hélène): the violent pride, the absolutism, the obsession with death, the disdain of mediocrity and the humdrum, the sense of her own uniqueness, emotional instability; but her unreal quality and her vengeful fury and lust for domination recall more particularly some of the more fearsome females of *The Second Sex*. She can be seen as another unedifying example of Beauvoirian womanhood, although the author did not create her with this intention.

It is ironic that Régine as an example of a narcissistic actress should be so dim, since in her autobiography Simone de Beauvoir sketches with marvelous brio the portrait of a real woman of this type, whom she calls Camille. In ten pages Camille emerges as a vivid and arresting character whom Simone de Beauvoir treats ironically and with humour. She connects her impressions of Camille with her own psychological doubts and failings of this period; she has twinges of envy, feelings of awe and inferiority in the presence of such a daring and prestigious creature; and the subtlety of her own self-analysis enhances the portrait of Camille. Sartre had discovered her and had been her admirer for two years. Simone de Beauvoir first hears his account of this bizarre and astonishing young woman long before she ever sets eyes on her: "As she had existed for me from afar she had the prestige of a heroine in a novel. She was beautiful with marvelous, thick blond hair, blue eyes, exquisite skin, a charming figure, perfect wrists and ankles." (LFDL'A, p. 77) Everything Camille does expresses the self-absorption and theatricality of a thorough-going narcissist, but she has amazing daring and "élan:" "She marvelled at her luck in combining so much beauty and intelligence in a single person and she felt that her kind of beauty and intelligence were utterly unique. She promised herself an exceptional fate." (LFDL'A, p. 77) Buried in the provinces, and bored with serious application to study and work although an avid reader and worshipper of the great ruthless figures: Lucifer, Blue Beard, Peter the Cruel, Caesar Borgia, Louis XI, Camille devotes her talents at first to "galanterie." (She becomes a high-class prostitute.) The account of this middle-class girl, stealthily slipping out of her house at night accompanied by a young gypsy to meet their "clients" at "élégantes maisons de rendez-vous" is captivating: "Camille had an acute sense of the importance of setting. While waiting for a client in the salon which was reserved for her, she would stand naked in front of the fireplace, with her long hair all loose and flowing, and she would be reading Michelet or later, Nietzsche. Her culture, her subtle ways of pleasing and her arrogance dazzled her notary and lawyer clients and they would weep with admiration on the pillow." (LFDL'A, p. 78) Everything she does is a theatrical performance. Her parties: "Camille presided over the banquet dressed as a patrician woman of decadent Rome, lying on a couch with Zina sitting at her feet." Her games and escapades: she and Zina dress up as beggars and wanly beg for alms around the cathedral. She meets Sartre at a funeral of a family of a mutual distant cousin. Simone de Beauvoir's description is delightful: "Sartre looked stiff in a black suit wearing a hat which belonged to his step-father which came down over his eyebrows; boredom extinguished all expression on his face and made him extravagantly ugly. Camille found him droll and she had a sudden inspiration, "He's Mirabeau," she said to herself." (LFDL'A, p. 79) Camille tires of her first role and does not find marriage to a "rich merchant of central heating" particularly exciting. "She had no more desire to become a respectable middle-class lady than she had to stay a prostitute." (LFDL'A, p. 79) What to do? Sartre convinces her that she must write, must create, in order to escape the mediocrity of the provinces; he will be her Pygmalion. She arrives in Paris but is disappointed with the grubbiness of the hotels, restaurants and dancings that Sartre's meagre funds provide. The job he found for her selling postcards in a stationery shop does not enrapture her. A heroine does not stoop to such menial necessities. She returns later on to Paris and attaches herself to Charles Dullin, who gives her small parts in his plays. Even being an actress interferes with her grandiose view of herself: "She took courses at the studio school and had parts in their plays; but she didn't feel she had an actress' vocation; she always refused to play characters in whom she didn't recognize herself; Agrippine, yes, but Junie, never. Furthermore, an actor's art is interpretative and really second best; she wanted to create." (LFDL'A, p. 81) She decides to write plays with roles worthy of her and contemplates a novel called "Histoires démoniaques." She throws dreadful scenes in rehearsal and continues to have dangerous and unnerving adventures with strange men whom she and Zina accost prowling around Montmartre at night. Camille is insatiable because reality is simply unable to furnish her with grandeur commensurate with her sublime gifts: "In spite of these diversions Camille found her life quite drab; she had never met anyone who seemed to reach her lofty altitude; the only equals she recognized were dead: Nietszche, Dürer, who according to one of his self-portraits looked a lot like her, and Emily Brontë, whom she had just discovered. She would have nocturnal rendezvous with them, she would talk to them and they would answer, after a certain fashion. When she regaled Sartre with her relations from beyond the tomb he would listen rather coldly." (LFDL'A, p. 81) When Simone de Beauvoir finally meets Camille the reality is somewhat less dazzling than the legend but, naïve and impressionable, the young Simone de Beauvoir is still hypnotized by this fabulous larger-than-life figure. She visits Camille, who is in exotic garb: long scarlet dressing gown opened over a white tunic, weighed down with jangling, antique jewelry, with her blond hair wound around her head and falling to her shoulders "in great twisted plaits in the medieval manner." Nietzsche, Dürer, and Emily Brontë look down on them from their frames on the wall and there are even two enormous dolls dressed as scholars whom Camille addresses affectionately as Friedrich and Albrecht. Camille is at once absurd and impressive with her stupefying showmanship although in many respects rather ordinary since her narcissistic pretensions play havoc with sincerity and generous feelings. She has the classic scorn for men who can be exploited and managed —mere puppets in effect—although she claims to be capable of grand and fatal passions. "What she expected of love was heart rending suffering followed by exalted reconciliations." Simone de Beauvoir is still under Camille's spell, but admits that she has an affected voice and irritating mannerisms. Furthermore, she speaks of love and men in a terribly cynical way: "She declared in the course of our conversation that a woman never has any difficulty in catching a man with her snares; a few theatrical scenes, a little flirtation, flattery, tact, and the game is up. I wouldn't admit that love finds its way through ruse and deception. For example, Camille herself wouldn't be able to succeed in manipulating Pagniez. 'Maybe,' she conceded disdainfully, 'But that's because he lacks passion and grandeur.' All the time she talked, she would play with her bracelets, touch her curls and dispatch tender little glances at herself in the mirror." (LFDL'A, p. 83) Camille reappears occasionally in the memoirs. Simone de Beauvoir finally recovers from her hero worship and recognizes a more mundane Camille, who is a blend of faults, virtues, and idiosyncracies. When one compares Régine with Camille, one is struck by the superior charm and vitality of the mere anecdotal reminiscences to the shadowy unreality of the novelistic entity.[4] Camille attracted Simone de Beauvoir because she seemed endowed with fictional grandeur, an unscrupulous heroine of epic dimensions, in spite of her inane affectations and absurdities which only added spice to the mixture. Judging from Camille, Simone de Beauvoir might have had a flair for "old-fashioned realism."[5]

More generally, however, Simone de Beauvoir is scathing about women writers who she says accept the world as it is and even glorify it, rummage in their precious childhoods for character, atmosphere, and themes, and write insipid, sentimental, anecdotal but popular novels. They are part of the plot to keep woman in her place since they exalt traditional womanhood. She describes them thus:

> they exalt the middle-class ideal of well-being and disguise the interests of their class in poetic colors; they orchestrate the grand mystification intended to persuade women to "stay womanly." Ancient houses, sheepfolds and kitchen gardens, picturesque old folks, roguish children, washing, preserving, family parties, toilettes, drawing-rooms, balls, unhappy but exemplary wives, the beauty of devotion and sacrifice, the small discontents and great joys of conjugal love, dreams of youth, the resignation of maturity—these themes the women novelists of England, France, America, Canada, and Scandinavia have exploited to their very dregs; they have thus gained fame and wealth, but have surely not enriched our vision of the world. [TSS, II, p. 667]

She then compares these writers to the great "rebels" like George Eliot, Jane Austen, the Brontës and Virginia Woolf, although she confuses subject matter and theme with artistic excellence.[6] Bad novels of revolt are altogether possible. It is true that this withering disdain for such sentimental "bourgeois" themes as suffering wives, ripe resignation, etc. is in accord with the general tenor of *The Second Sex,* where family "devotion" and domesticity are considered tepid vegetating.

Worshipping great artists as a young woman, Simone de Beauvoir admires and envies Camille for the dogged hard work which she does finally expend on her creative efforts—she stays up half the night or rises at dawn to write furiously. "Camille marched with sure steps towards fame," says a spellbound Simone de Beauvoir. After all artistic creation is not pure disinterested asceticism; even the great male artists have almost all felt that 'fame is the spur.' " Simone de Beauvoir herself is not immune to "la gloire." In fact, her whole adverse judgment on the female sex stems in part from her feeling that woman is barred by her traditional role and feminine psychology from experiencing the restless, insatiable, Faustian ambition that has spurred on the great creative spirits. In contrast, Simone de Beauvoir describes Camille's first ascension to the heights when Dullin produces a play she herself had written and in which she has the leading role. The theme of the play is patently autobiographical except that the principal character, "an extremely beautiful and exceptional woman" is cast in a romantic medieval setting, in Toulouse, Camille's hometown. "La belle pharmacienne" deserts her boring husband for a splendid "grand seigneur" and the play is all exalted passion and renouncement. Unhappily it was badly received and even laughed off the stage. Simone de Beauvoir recounts: "Camille was resplendent and she played her part with such conviction that she compelled our sympathy. However, when she writhed on the ground howling, 'I wanted to bite ravenously into the lymphatic flesh of life,' the audience burst out laughing; at the end of the play the curtain fell amid tumultuous boo's." (LFDL'A, p. 124) Simone de Beauvoir's feelings about Camille's defeat are much more charitable and more aware of the complexity of human motivation and endeavor than her strictures on women artists in *The Second Sex*. She does not regard this defeat as necessarily reprehensible, but she does feel that the play was annoyingly narcissistic in theme and in its absurd exaltation of the heroine as a self-portrait of Camille. She concludes that the failure stems not from lack of talent or application but from Camille's incapacity for self-criticism. There is an implicit conviction in Simone de Beauvoir's writings that such obstacles as lack of talent could always be vanquished by trying harder, being less self-centered, etc. She takes her "freedom" seriously. And thus Simone de Beauvoir does not consign Camille to the nether regions of hollow artists so pitilessly dealt with in *The Second Sex.*

In a discussion of actresses in *Le Deuxième Sexe* Simone de Beauvoir points out that the great woman actresses, singers, and dancers have been singularly lucky because they have been able to transcend their feminine role in a creative way while at the same time maintaining and even accentuating their "femininity." In fulfilling themselves as human beings, they fulfill themselves as women because even in their work they are supposed to be beautiful, admired, sexually attractive, etc. All the dangers of narcissistic pitfalls are doubled, however, and it is characteristic of Simone de Beauvoir to conclude this section on a critical note, implying that in general actresses, dancers, and singers are somehow morally suspect. If they are not Rachel or Duse, they owe this to their failings as women. The following description has many affinities with the real history of Camille, but it ends with a harsh generalization about actresses and singers which betrays the habitual anti-feminine tone of this book:

> But, above all, the admiration she feels for her ego in many cases limits the achievement of an actress; she has such illusions regarding the value of her mere presence that serious work seems useless. She is concerned above all to put herself in the public eye and sacrifices the character she is interpreting to this theatrical quackery ["cabotinage"]. She also lacks the generous-mindedness to forget herself, and this deprives her of the possibility of going beyond herself; rare indeed are the Rachels, the Duses, who avoid this reef and make their persons the instruments of their art instead of seeing in art a servant of

their egos. In her private life, moreover, the bad actress ["cabotine"] will exaggerate all the narcissistic defects: she will reveal herself as vain, petulant, theatric; she will consider all the world a stage. [TSS, II, p. 662]

Why does Simone de Beauvoir switch from "actrice" to the pejorative "cabotine"? In spite of her insistence that the "situation" accounts for all this, one has a dark suspicion that the feminine tendencies toward weakness and perversity are stubbornly entrenched in the very nature of things.

NOTES

1. Contemporary feminist criticism is justly unsparing of the inhuman mess male-dominated cultures have made of sex. Man has projected his own guilt about sexuality upon woman and from the Old Testament on she has been an evil temptress and sexual snare. The sexual double standard is symbolic of man's inhuman treatment of woman.

2. Paule forgives Henri all his transient, superficial infidelities; she accepts this as the price of keeping him and convinces herself that such pecadillos cannot touch their "grand amour."

3. Joé Bousquet, "Simone de Beauvoir et la poésie," *Critique,* no. 12 (May 1947), 390–93.

4. Simone de Beauvoir and Sartre admired Hemingway and the simplicity of his style. "He conformed to our philosophical requirements. Old-fashioned realism which describes objects in themselves depended on false premises. Proust and Joyce chose, each in his own fashion, to use a subjectivism which we considered just as ill-founded." (LFDL'A, p. 159) Readers of novels seem never to tire of characters who have fictional vitality. Camille has the potentialities of such a character. Though based on a real person with a natural appendage of fascinating eccentricities, she emerges as an imaginary figure distorted by Simone de Beauvoir's imagination and youthful credulity.

5. In her discussion of *L'Invitée* Simone de Beauvoir explains her esthetic doctrine and the influence of Hemingway and her distaste for descriptive realism." "Of all the influences I've felt Hemingway's is the most evident and several critics have pointed this out. One of the qualities of his writing that I've appreciated the most is his refusal to make supposedly objective

descriptions: landscape, scenes and objects are always presented through the hero's eyes as he is affected by the action. I tried to do the same thing. I also sought to imitate as he did the tone and rhythm of spoken language without fearing repetitions and banalities." (LFDL'A, p. 396)

6. Whereas Jane Austen, for example, hardly a "rebel," has extremely unpromising, unexciting subject matter, just as "feminine" as can be imagined (who is going to marry whom), but her artistry transforms it. All great artists are perhaps "rebels" if only in the sense that they make us see profoundly and question the basic fabric of existence.

5

Girls

XAVIÈRE OF *L'INVITÉE* AND NADINE OF *LES MANDARINS*

In *The Second Sex* Simone de Beauvoir devotes several long chapters to woman's "formation," i.e., training, education, or molding of character. She attempts to show the complex manner in which familial, social, biological, and cultural influences subtly combine to make the life of a girl more difficult than that of a boy. Her conditioning, according to *The Second Sex,* produces profound psychological estrangement but is also instrumental in making her accept her inferior status as the inessential "object." As usual, Simone de Beauvoir presents a staggering amount of material, argues every side of the question, and lists the compensations as well as the trials of a feminine upbringing. Yet the main theme remains that young girls are subject to influences which inhibit their full human development and which encourage encourage timidity, passivity, and evasion. This leads to the "resignation" of the adult woman who accepts docilely the traditional role for which biology and culture have destined her. There is the usual mixture of penetrating acumen, sound common sense, brilliant aphorisms, bewildering contradictions, over-simplifications, and fatiguing exaggerations.

150

The discussion of "la jeune fille" and her "femininity" is generally somber. Women are taught since childhood and learn through bitter experience that independence and self-assertion are not regarded as alluring by the male and that they must repress such natural impulses and coyly feign passivity and deference to the male. Women must above all please, and to please means to conform to masculine prejudices of how women should be. Generally speaking, men have appalling taste in this matter, . . . "men do not like *garçons manqués* (tomboys), or blue-stockings, or brainy women; too much daring, culture, or intelligence, too much character, will frighten them." (TSS, II, p. 314) Any woman with a modicum of intelligence recognizes with pleasure this depressing masculine syndrome and Simone de Beauvoir's amusing observation that it is usually the vapid, stupid, clinging little wisp of a creature who wins the hero in novels is an admirable illustration of the deplorable ordinariness of male tastes. As George Eliot said it is the "blond and stupid heroine" who wins the man. Simone de Beauvoir recounts in her autobiography that she never quite recovered from the shock that Laurie in *Little Women* does not pick the dashing and sympathetic Jo but rather "the insipid Amy with the curly hair." All of this is very engaging and contains a germ of profound and tragic truth except that there are other heroines that contradict this thesis and that aren't mentioned, like Stendhal's for instance.[1]

The young girl finds she must repress all naturalness, spontaneity, and wildness and develop the studied arts of pleasing men which means she must cultivate docility and "charm": she must at all costs be ladylike. "Any self-assertion will diminish her femininity and her attractiveness." (TSS, II, p. 314) Now all of this is true, in a way, and present-day feminists are implacable and richly sardonic about the absurd "feminine ideal" that young adolescent girls are so conditioned to strive for. (I remember now with amazement the advice to teen-age girls in women's magazines telling us with perfect aplomb "to be sure to *always* talk about HIM." Incredible. And we actually followed this advice!) It's funny and tragic both, because the spectacle of gifted and intelligent people actually feigning stupidity and dreading success so as not to frighten away *men* is a hideous commentary on centuries of male-domination. (I've often wondered how civilization has survived or at least not grown dangerously moronic due to the ingrained masculine superiority syndrome that dictates that no man could tolerate a wife more intelligent or even as intelligent as himself. What a mockery of enlightened genetics!) Still, Simone de Beauvoir exaggerates. Men are (strangely enough) also attracted to women who have strength of character, dash, talent, originality, wit, and *even* intelligence because these are obviously attractive human qualities and women are after all human beings (aren't they?). Simone de Beauvoir's lurid conception of what it means to be "feminine" wrenches this word from its other meanings which also include many favorable connotations. All women, including Simone de Beauvoir, wish to be thought "feminine" (except of course when the term is used pejoratively which is alas too often the case), so it cannot be a completely undesirable state, implying vapidity, weakness, and surrender.

The leitmotiv of woman's malediction reappears throughout the study of the young girl. Young girls are prone to hypochondria and internal disorders, but this is induced by the nefarious social attitudes which inhibit their natural vivacity and encourage morbid concern with bodily aches and pains. The abstract young girls of

The Second Sex sound a good deal closer to Elsie Dins-
more than the young girl of the present day. There is a
faint aroma of smelling salts and fainting fits alien to
contemporary reality. At this stage Simone de Beauvoir
says she is still an autonomous human being; she is subject, not object; but she is doomed to become that extremely bound and limited creature, a wife and mother.
"To become feminine" is the equivalent of defeat. In
becoming a woman the young girl somehow becomes a
lesser human being. If one accepts being "the other,"
one must inexorably renounce one's real selfhood and
exist as an inessential, derivative, lesser human being.
Here again woman's "situation" has pernicious effects
upon her character. Young girls, like adult women, are
exceptionally prone to "lying," "ruse," "bad faith." Yet
Simone de Beauvoir is much more sympathetic to young
girls because they have not yet succumbed to their ig-
nominious fate, and often display admirable amounts of
fierce independence, spontaneity, orginality, exhuberance, and generosity. But her future looms darkly. To
become an adult is difficult, but for the young girl it
assumes tragic dimensions and the intemperate language
of *The Second Sex* with its extremes of "prey," "rape,"
"passivity," etc. etc. transforms what is universal and
natural into a nightmare of equally repellent alternatives.

Mémoires d'une Jeune Fille Rangée brilliantly evokes Simone de Beauvoir's childhood and adolescence and cap-
tures the atmosphere of a particular social class and milieu in a particular time and place. The adolescence of
Simone de Beauvoir rendered so entertainingly in this
book is quite unlike the account of "la jeune fille" in *The
Second Sex.* The young Simone de Beauvoir in spite of her
adolescent anguish, doubts, "crises de nerfs," affinities
for "le nouveau mal du siècle," and vertiginious descents

into gloom about the nothingness of all things, was fundamentally spirited, gifted, optimistic, and energetic young girl who would in no way qualify as a mournful representative of "the second sex," doomed to passivity and servitude. In fact the dominant note of Simone de Beauvoir's adolescence is one of liberation and plenitude, despite the fluctuations of mood common to that age. The book concludes with a veritable triumph since this young girl, product of an obscure and intellectually undistinguished Catholic girls' school, "Le Cours Désir," competes successfully with the most brilliant lycée-trained boys of her own age and wins a coveted "agrégation" in philosophy. Simone de Beauvoir's "camarades" or equals when she first tries teaching in a lycée are Lévi-Strauss and Merleau-Ponty!

Simone de Beauvoir affirms that she herself did not feel torn by searing conflicts between her own worth as a human being and her femininity. She appears to have felt at ease in both masculine and feminine domains and her own successful leap into a preponderantly masculine sphere was invigorating and exhilarating. The attitude of the young men toward her success was the antithesis of the dour male disapproval of such feminine intellectual effrontery which *The Second Sex* delineates so piquantly. "I certainly didn't regret being a woman; on the contrary, I derived great satisfaction from it. My education had convinced me of the intellectual inferiority of my sex and most of my feminine fellow students agreed." (MD'UJFR, 284) However, Simone de Beauvoir transcends this natural handicap and it becomes even an advantage since for a woman at that time (or any other) her attainment was a prodigious feat. The young men did not see her as a rival but treated her with good humor and camaraderie without condescension. She describes her treatment by her male colleagues: "I was proud of having won their esteem; their kindness meant I could avoid that "challenging" attitude which was to annoy me later in American women: from the very first men were for me comrades and not adversaries. Far from envying them, I found my own position as an intellectual woman a privileged one because of the fact that it was so unusual and so rare." (MD'UJFR, p. 284)[2] In fact, she has the best of both possible worlds because her intellectual attainments in no way impair her femininity in the eyes of others or herself. Although she and her sister are "badly dressed" they apply great care to their looks and their clothes; Simone de Beauvoir has been told she is pretty and her feminine friends regard her as one of them, a full-fledged "feminine" being. Moreover she has a special affection for her feminine friends whom she regards as in many ways superior to the young men. They have characteristic feminine problems and failings, but Simone de Beauvoir is sympathetic; it does not occur to her to judge their foibles because they are "feminine." "On many points I placed Zaza, my sister, Stepha and even Lisa above my masculine friends; more sensitive and more generous, they were better equipped to recognize the worth of dreams, tears and love. I flattered myself that I combined in fine proportion "the heart of a woman" and "the brains of a man." (MD'UJFR, p. 288) Thus it is difficult at first to account for the extremism of *The Second Sex* which holds that one's "femininity" and one's vital personal autonomy and independence are basically at odds with one another, when the author's own experience of this supposedly crippling division was by her account so untroubled. Simone de Beauvoir would no doubt say that she had chosen "transcendence" in renouncing woman's traditional role and thus was spared her cruel and limiting fate. All the same, the pessimistic theory and somber emotive atmosphere of *The Second Sex* carry a sense of conviction about woman's malediction that seems "felt" and not just abstractly concocted from disinterested observations of other women's woes.

There are other indications in the autobiography though that suggest the origin of the theory. Simone de Beauvoir grew up in a world where boys were privileged and where the feminine sphere was preponderantly suffocating, drab, and domestic. Her father was in her eyes a much more interesting and vital person than her mother despite her gradual disillusionment with the childhood divinity he represented. As a small child she admired everything about him: "My father was astonished by the paradoxes of human feeling, by heredity, by the strangeness of dreams; I never saw my mother astonished by anything." (MD'UJFR, p. 39) Simone de Beauvoir's younger sister was vaguely disappointing to the family because she was not a boy. Simone de Beauvoir describes her: "She was called Poupette; she was two-and-a-half years younger than I. Everyone said she looked like Papa. Blonde, with blue eyes, in her baby pictures her expression seems to be misted over with tears. Her birth had been a disappointment because the whole family wanted a boy; certainly no one bore her a personal grudge for being a girl; but perhaps it wasn't entirely propitious for her that people had longed for a boy in her place." (MD'UJFR, p. 43) Later when Simone de Beauvoir was an adolescent she got used to remarks from her father and mother like "Too bad Simone isn't a boy—she could have gone to the Polytechnique!" A vague impression that boys were more important hovered in the air, but all girls get that impression and it isn't somehow too debilitating. Simone de Beauvoir envies her cousin Jacques' privileged freedom. He can read any book he wants to, go to nightclubs and have mysterious adventures while all the books in Simone de Beauvoir's house have forbidden clipped passages and her mother even reads her daughters' letters with self-righteous complacency. Simone de Beauvoir does not even set foot in a café until she is twenty years old, and on this thrilling occasion Jacques brings her home at 2 A.M., which provokes a dire familial crisis. In the practical sphere it *was* in many respects a malediction to be a girl.

No doubt the equivocal and unjust attitude of Simone de Beauvoir's father toward her future which he had himself ordained for her must have been incomprehensible and deeply wounding. His ruinous investments meant that his daughters would have no dowry and thus must become self-supporting, which conformed miraculously well with Simone de Beauvoir's own inclinations: necessity was a blessing in disguise. However, his ambiguous cruelty and ill-disguised contempt left permanent scars. The fatal opposition between one's human value and one's femininity that dominates *The Second Sex* is almost exactly echoed in the cruel and obscurantist attitudes of Simone de Beauvoir's father. Despite his literary inclination and his wit and charm, Simone de Beauvoir's father shared the reactionary prejudices of his class so that, furiously anti-feminist and admirer of "la vraie femme," Simone de Beauvoir's studies and ambitions paradoxically lessened her value in his eyes. She couldn't exactly understand then his ambivalent attitudes but she felt them painfully. He would ignore her efforts and progress in school and then rave significantly about his brother's daughter who was not intellectual but "feminine" and sweet. His lack of sympathy had complicated causes and was in part due to his impaired self-esteem that his financial failures caused. His intellectual daughter represented defeat because she would have to work for a living. Simone de Beauvoir analyzes succintly the kind of spurious familial love that bourgeois parents like her father often demonstrate toward their children who are valued more as decoration of the parental ego than as individual human beings to be valued for their own sake. Her skepticism about the authenticity of familial affection so pronounced in *The Second Sex* has in her case a heartfelt validity. Her father would actually complain openly about the sacrifices which his daughters cost him and give them the impression that they imposed upon his charity. Indeed the irrational attitudes of Simone de Beauvoir's father toward her because she was in fact successful at what he had himself planned for her were very galling and painful. She did therefore in some way experience inchoate divisions in herself since she tried to please her father and in so doing earned his disdain and hostility. It was enough to produce trauma in anyone. She describes her feelings:

> I obviously didn't realize the contradiction which tormented my father: but I quickly realized the one in my own situation. I conformed exactly to his wishes: and yet he seemed offended by this; he was the one who had encouraged me to study, yet he reproached me for having my face always buried in a book. You would have thought, judging from his morose expression, that I had committed myself against his will to a vocation which he had in fact chosen for me himself. I would wonder what I was guilty of; I felt uncomfortable about myself and I had bitterness in my heart. [MD'UJFR, p. 173]

Even though Simone de Beauvoir comes to realize her father's very marked human limitations, such cruel and unjust devaluation helps to explain her extreme rejection of the traditional concept of "femininity" which her father so fatuously admired. Now, with Simone de Beauvoir and her account of "la jeune fille" in mind, let us look at fictional representatives.

Two of Simone de Beauvoir's more arresting fictional feminine characters, Xavière of *L'Invitée* and Nadine of *Les Mandarins,* are young girls on the brink of adulthood. They may be considered as autonomous fictional characters in Simone de Beauvoir's imaginative world and one can also observe how they demonstrate, if they do, Simone de Beauvoir's ideas about "la jeune fille" in *The Second Sex.* Xavière Pagès of *L'Invitée* is one of Simone de Beauvoir's most beguiling feminine characters. She is such a successful invention that even her unattractive qualities contribute to her considerable charm as a splendidly realized fictional creation. Sullen, jealous, capricious, unreasonable, and above all inscrutable, she has the power to annoy and irritate but also to astonish. Dominique Aury refers to her as "the odious Xavière" which is not altogether inexact, but her stubborn defiance and childish perversity are part of her fictional vitality.

The character of Xavière was inspired by Simone de Beauvoir's young friend Olga Kosakievicz, whose sympathetic portrait she sketches in *La Force de L'Age.* However, Simone de Beauvoir systematically transforms Olga into a quite different and self-contained fictional character. The way in which an artist transmutes life into art is always somewhat mysterious, and Simone de Beauvoir's account of the transmogrification of Olga into Xavière is instructive:

> I used Olga as an inspiration for the composition of Xavière in *L'Invitée* but I did this by systematically distorting the real Olga's attitudes. The conflict which pitted my two heroines

against each other couldn't have developed any real bite if I hadn't endowed Xavière with unrelenting, cunning selfishness beneath her charming surface. Olga certainly was capricious, moody and inconsistent but this side of her was only her most superficial aspect. . . . When I invented Xavière I only retained the myth that we had formed around Olga which was only faintly related to the living person, and in doing that I de-glamorized the myth considerably. [LFDL'A, p. 278–79]

Thus Xavière is a highly distilled version of the real Olga, who was herself deformed by two irrepressible novelist-philosophers who could not resist subjecting their real friends to fanciful philosophic interpretations.[3] Like Olga with Simone de Beauvoir and Sartre, Xavière resents and resists Pierre's and Françoise's mania for interpretation; their relentless character analysis provokes her furious resistance. In fact, the whole scheme of the novel is built upon Xavière's stubborn resistance to their efforts to elucidate and explain her motives. They analyze, interpret, and hypothesize interminably about Xavière's every word and gesture but are ultimately unable to capture the secret of her inner self which forever eludes them. Simone de Beauvoir reinforces this sense of Xavière's ultimate mystery, intrinsic to the theme of the novel, by presenting her from the outside. Xavière's consciousness is undisclosed to the reader.

Xavière's appealing traits are borrowed from Olga, and to read Simone de Beauvoir's anecdotes about Olga is to receive a more fully documented version of Xavière's captivating side. We have less information about Xavière than Olga, but our impression of her is strong because she is at the center of a well-wrought novel where the conflict between the characters is designed to produce reaction. Yet to describe Olga's particular charm is in a sense to describe Xavière. Blonde, pretty, vivacious, intelligent, sensitive, at eighteen Olga is "against almost everything." Furiously uncompromising, impetuous, ardent, naïvely admiring, intense, loftily scornful of stuffiness, given to violent extremes, candid and sincere, she is very fetching, especially in the anecdotes where her qualities are dramatized. Her naïveté and spontaneity emerge for instance in the episode about the violinist. Daughter of Russian exiles, Olga asks Simone de Beauvoir what it means to be a Jew, and Simone de Beauvoir who was as she says at this period "deplorably abstract" answers: "Nothing. Jews don't exist; only men exist." Armed with this knowledge, Olga dashes into the room of a fellow boarder, a Jewish violinist, and announces, "My friend, you don't exist! My professor of philosophy told me so!" When Olga reads Stendhal and Proust she speaks of them with rapture or rage because she responds to books as though they were living people. She is the antithesis of the judicious, critical, rational, calculating mind: she is all passion and impulsiveness, but captivating. Here is Simone de Beauvoir on Olga, which is an effective backdrop for Xavière:

. . . Without understanding everything about it, she was still rarely mistaken about the quality of a person or a book. She possessed that quality that we regarded as essential: authenticity: she never faked her opinions or her impressions. She had something impetuous and extreme about her which won me over completely. . . . . Olga would give herself up to pleasure with total abandon: sometimes she would dance until she fainted dead away. She observed everything, especially people, with avid intensity. This wonder before the world preserved her childlike freshness; she would often sit dreaming for hours enrapt by heaven knows what wondrous visions. I also liked the way she would behave and express herself with the most delicate tact and discretion even though I knew that her polished manners encased a brooding, fiery temperament. [LFDL'A, p. 266]

Despite Olga's gifts she is in a state of adolescent disequilibrium: she is frenetically volatile, lacks all discipline, and is unable to concentrate on long-range projects, is defeatist and easily despondent at failure. Simone de Beauvoir and Sartre decide she might study philosophy, but the first day she must write a résumé on a chapter of Bergson she swallows a box of erasers which naturally incapacitates her for further work. "In fact, abstract speculation hardly interested her at all."

Xavière has the same blonde, fragile prettiness, the same passionate intensity, droll and delicate imagination, aristocratic disdain, furious intransigeance, haughty contempt for "le sérieux," and the same sad-little-waif quality as Olga, but her childish capriciousness is exaggerated so that it quite often becomes downright malevolence and annoying infantile selfishness. Her engaging freshness and charm are always in precarious balance with her ill-humored imperiousness. She often behaves so petulantly and unreasonably that Pierre's and Françoise's tolerance of this spoiled child seems excessive, but they are clearly bewitched. The other characters see their fascination with Xavière as comic, and this radical difference in perspective, such a commonplace in life, is exactly what Simone de Beauvoir intends to emphasize.

Xaviere's character is sketched in delicate traits in her first appearance. She feels dispirited because her bleak future in Rouen looms up as an absolute desert but since she has no skill or métier and is, in fact, quite incompetent, she must bow to necessity and return to her parents in the provinces. She treats her dire situation in a droll and insouciant way. She humorously suggests that though not too gifted she might become a prostitute; she would really work hard at learning the trade and her charming naïveté shows through all of her remarks intended to be daring and cynical, since she admits she couldn't even bring herself to accept the sailor who invites her to dance. She shows Françoise a drawing she has made of a bespangled woman who vaguely resembles Françoise and which she has entitled in huge violet letters, "the way to vice". Françoise urges her to take energetic action to avert her dismal fate: she even offers to help Xavière financially until she finds work. Xavière is stubbornly opposed to doing anything whatsoever and shows a healthy distaste for boring work, but also a very childish reluctance to be responsible for herself. Françoise struggles with her manfully, sympathetic to a fault. All her suggestions produce aversion in Xavière, who recoils from stenography, modeling, and all practical mundane jobs as well as more glamorous study in theatre or art. When Françoise sensibly points out that a few hours of some boring work might be worth the price of her independence, Xavière responds with absolutist disdain: "I hate these loathesome compromises. If you can't have the life you want, you shouldn't have to live it." When asked what *would* appeal to her, she becomes dreamy and poetic and conjures up some golden moments in her childhood—riding horseback at dawn with her father when the world seemed magical and new. She has impeccable taste and knows what is important in life but her sense of realism is nil. She registers imperious disdain for those who accept the necessity and compromise of daily existence. It is impossible to deal with this irrational and peevish child. Françoise discerns that Xavière's pride has been injured because her offer to help Xavière financially seemed like humiliating charity. Her bewildering changes of mood and strange mixture of pride and humble childish deference are perplexing but attract Francoise and make her a willing accomplice and victim.

Xavière's equivocal charm envelops and fascinates Françoise and Pierre and is in large part responsible for the tortuous imbroglio the trio becomes since Xavière's almost oriental inscrutability and enigmatic behavior stimulate their over-developed imaginations. They batten on her shifting moods, childish whims, and inexplicable rancors, although they all suffer as a result of this unhealthy kind of emotional vampirism. Xavière's charm always contains an acid, negative aftertaste and her haughtiness and contempt for ordinary people has a very unpleasant, uncharitable side. At such moments the prestige she retains in the eyes of Françoise and Pierre seems misplaced. She visits Françoise at the sanitorium and her arrogance about the nurse plus her insidiously cruel treatment of Françoise reveals that this elfin charm exists simultaneously with a cruel and hateful egoism. One often wants to wring Xavière's neck. She regales the invalid Françoise with picturesque accounts of her adventures in cafés with Pierre. She tells about her absurd, light-hearted flirtations with eccentric habitués of the café. It is all wondrously droll, but Françoise feels her enthusiasm dampened somehow. Xavière is like that; her good qualities have negative reverberations. What bothers Françoise is not Xavière's gift for flirtation but her complacency about it. A nurse comes in and gives Françoise a shot and Xavière, annoyed by this intrusion, sullenly looks out the window during the operation. When the nurse departs Xavière bursts out violently about this "horrible good woman" and asks how anyone could *ever be* a nurse. Her indignation is stimulated by her childish horror of shots. Yet she manages to include Françoise in her scorn and succeeds in making her feel that being sick is something somehow disgraceful. She lacks human empathy. Her revolt against the human condition has its puerile and sinister side since her superior disdain often makes other people feel wretched. She somehow makes Françoise feel old, ugly, and positively ashamed of being sick. Xavière often behaves unspeakably and is given to violent excess. She throws scenes at parties, drinks too much, remains locked up in her room for hours at a time without so much as reading a book, takes ether, burns her hand in a melodramatic gesture of stoical self-contempt, but always manages to carry off these stormy performances with an air of superiority. These antics prove she is true to herself; they represent the quintessential Xavière.

Xavière exhibits the qualities of adolescent intransigeance and revolt which *The Second Sex* depicts. Simone de Beauvoir's young girl is attractive in her rejection of social conformity and her all-or-nothing idealism which scorns the sordid compromises of life and dreams of grandeur, splendid accomplishment, and a purer, better world. Yet all her daring and moral superiority are based on dreams as she is in reality pathetically powerless and excluded from action. But she is fetching and in many ways more sensitive and superior to adolescent boys because of the real limitations of her existence which paradoxically encourage some of the best qualities which are essentially those that children have. As *The Second Sex* puts it: "Because she does not act, she observes, she feels, she records; a color, a smile awakens profound echoes within her. . . . Being poorly integrated in the universe of humanity and hardly able to adapt herself therein, she, like the child, is able to see it objectively." (TSS, II, p. 339) The unattractive qualities of young girls are also dealt with at great length and they too stem from the difficult situation of being on the threshold of a secondary, inauthentic existence; the girl must resign herself to a circumscribed, domestic sphere just at an age when the future should appear the most glorious. Because being rather than doing is her lot she suffers vaguely and these frustrations inspire bizarre and foolish behavior: she runs away from home, makes up stories, dramatizes her life, and is secretive, moody, and untruthful. Certainly Xavière fits *The Second Sex* abstract formula for "la jeune fille." However, the comparison seems somewhat irrelevant and it is difficult to see her strictly in terms of a young girl frustrated by her feminine condition. For Xavière with all of her violence and negation is especially memorable for her stalwart affirmation of herself. No one would dare to call Xavière an "object" with impunity. This is precisely why Pierre and Françoise are so impressed with her; she doesn't care what people think; she stubbornly is what she is; she boldly affirms her own inviolate and precious identity. Of course, actually, Xavière is a pathetic, childish, and dependent young girl, a parasite really, with an appalling lack of responsibility; yet her tenacious insistence on her own frivolous values enthralls Pierre and Françoise. They try to reason with Xavière, but she maddeningly frustrates their attempts. Though no doubt masking her feelings of inadequacy and helplessness, she insists on being herself, no matter how indolent or unproductive. Much of this is a pose no doubt, but all the same this defiant affirmation of self is in fact intrinsic to the theme of the novel; Françoise's suffering and jealousy are cruelly exacerbated by her sense that, ironically, this feather-weight girl without any serious claim to excellence should be so confident and thus compel Pierre's admiration.

In this sense Xavière does not conform to *The Second Sex's* theories about the young girl caught in the tormenting tug-of-war between her own authentic self and her future inauthentic being as the inessential other. *L'Invitée* was written six years before *The Second Sex* and shows little trace of Simone de Beauvoir's preoccupation with the woman question. In existentialist terms Xavière has the "being" that Françoise lacks, a complete reversal of *The Second Sex* since Xavière does nothing and Françoise is admirably energetic and resourceful. Xavière is all self-affirmation which in no way impairs her feminine attractiveness; in fact this is the source of her attraction. She is intensely feminine but hardly docile or passive. However, she does exhibit the kind of characteristic behavior which is always condemned severely in *The Second Sex:* she insists on *being;* it doesn't matter what she *does* as long as she *is* Xavière. According to *The Second Sex* this is an intensely feminine attitude and women are perpetually reproached for preferring being to transcendence, although these categories become rather slippery and arbitrary. Yet this attitude, as embodied in the character of Xavière, has a certain power and validity because for all her iniquitous charm and futile behavior she does compel respect by her sheer presence and force. The spell she casts on Françoise and Pierre attests to her considerable power. Xaviere's independence of character does not depend on action or work.[4] Her stubborn individuality and ambivalent stance of fierce truthfulness and jealous conniving do not seem explicable in terms of her feminine condition. Besides Simone de Beauvoir always insists on her authenticity, her firm selfhood, etc. Xavière is a stunning example of baffling human impenetrability, though certainly her helpless situation as a young girl "sans métier" does affect her behavior.

She continues to charm Françoise and Pierre in spite of her infuriating egoism. Xavière has recently staged an appalling self-immolation scene where, without flinching, she applied a lighted cigarette to her hand in a nightclub. Pierre and Xavière's mutual admiration and witty exchanges fail to elicit Françoise's customary enthusiasm although Xavière is in her habitual good form. She makes charming little poetic "aperçus" about Pierre. She continues to embroider little fancies about Pierre which charm him immeasurably but reveal that underneath this dreamy exterior Xavière has a hard inner core of savage possessiveness. Françoise realizes with horror at the end of this evening that Xavière is in reality full of rage and jealousy because she cannot succeed in completely tearing Pierre away from Françoise. Pierre's least little attention and kindness to Françoise destroy all Xavière's gay exhuberance and she becomes taciturn and sullen. As the disintegrating trio envelops all three members in a tortuous barrage of destructive emotions, Xavière becomes less and less endearing and reveals hitherto unsuspected depths of duplicity, envy and hatred. All the same, Xavière's very contradictions are part of her considerable fictional charm. Furthermore, all the characters disintegrate, revealing dark proclivities and they inflict shocking verbal violence on each other. By contrast, Xavière often seems sad, childishly vulnerable, and utterly pathetic, as when Pierre attacks her pitilessly, unmasking her every treacherous motive. At this moment she claims our sympathy because she is the victim of Pierre's unjust attack; he too has exploited Xavière in an inhuman and obtuse way. Xaviere's ignoble reaction to the trio is in principle no more contemptible than Françoise's jealousy. She is a good extentialist moralist; she defines her own values and splendidly adheres to her own self-interest. She often insinuates that she is superior to Françoise because she is a free creature not shackled by noble considerations of self-mutilating altruism.[5] Pierre and Françoise are inclined to be self-righteous and often talk as though they were morally impeccable, especially Pierre in this harrowing scene, but their treatment of Xavière has its own sinister and exploitative side. In the thick miasma of emotions the trio engenders, all the characters suffer a sea change. But Xavière retains her perverse individuality and remains one of Simone de Beauvoir's most arresting fictional characters. Her forlorn little-girl wistfulness and childish temperamental excesses could no doubt be chalked up to the inner conflicts caused by a young girl's inadaptability to the cruel world. In the end, though, she resists sociological and psychological explanation (although she is perhaps intended to have a metaphysical one) and rests implacably and inscrutably Xavière, a worthy member of Simone de Beauvoir's feminine fictional gallery with all the negative violence so characteristic of Beauvoirian femininity, but unlike the sad troop of wretched neurotic women, incontestably and indomitably herself.

Simone de Beauvoir has created in Nadine of *Les Mandarins* another young girl who has her own furious individuality and who yet exhibits characteristic features of Beauvoirian femininity. She is divided within herself, unhappy and painfully ill-adopted to her environment which on the surface is benign and ostensibly designed to encourage her happiness and self-fulfillment. However, Nadine is restless and self-destructive, bitterly contentious and negative, and full of unsuppressed hostility toward her mother, with whom she erupts upon occasion

with a torrent of vituperation in language heavily laced
with obscenities. As Dominique Aury says, the language
of all the characters in *Les Mandarins* often suggest that
of *La Série Noire.* The intellectuals in it love gutter talk,[6]
especially Nadine, whose antics are continually diverting
by dint of their sheer violence and contrariness. Nadine
behaves most of the time with so little grace and charm
that one marvels at the patience and affection of Lambert
and Henri, both of whom are mysteriously attracted by
her unusual blend of youthful fragility and ferocity.

Simone de Beauvoir's extended analysis of *Les Mandarins* in *La Force des Choses* includes an account of the
genesis of the character of Nadine with whom she took
great pains. Her initial impulse was to endow Nadine
with some of the unbeguiling aggressive traits of young
women she had known, notably Lise Oblanoff, a white
Russian student and friend, and to try to show the
complicated psychological dynamics of such behavior.
Nadine's furious contrariness is well rendered, and her
childish petulance, unamiable verbal assaults and kill-joy
bad humor are impressively evoked. However, there are
mitigating touches and the author's sympathy makes Nadine something more complex than a one-dimensional
fury.

One instantly recognizes in Lise Oblanoff, who appears in the autobiography, some affinity with Nadine,
both in her original character traits and in some of the
events of her life. However, Lise is treated briefly, anec-
dotally, and rather superficially and her astonishing excesses are related in a humorous and tolerant way. She
does not approach the malignant, neurotic intensity of
the fictionally finished Nadine. Simone de Beauvoir borrows some of Lise's features, develops, transforms and
exaggerates them and arrives at something quite *sui gen-*

eris by "darkening" somewhat her original inspiration just as in the case of Olga-Xavière. Lise is a white Russian, a pupil of Simone de Beauvoir's, seventeen years old, blonde, somewhat gauche and unstylishly dressed who suffers from her expatriate status which exacerbates her aggressive hostility toward the world. Like Nadine, she studies chemistry without enthusiasm and like Nadine she is extraordinarily aggressive and haughty, given to astounding eccentricities and whims. She is lonely and has no friend, since her one congenial Russian companion was forced to leave school. Nadine likewise has no feminine friend she can confide in. Lise's isolation and loneliness encourage pride and lofty contempt. Her equivocal situation as an exile and her humor and imagination recall Olga-Xavière more than Nadine, whose sense of humor and fanciful imagination are not highly developed. Lise shares Nadine's penchant for outrageous behavior, which both attracted and annoyed Simone de Beauvoir. We are treated to several diverting examples of Lise's scandalous behavior—"Entering a church to admire it, she washed her hands in the holy water fount." This desire to shock is equally pronounced in Nadine. Simone de Beauvoir describes the battle of wills between herself and Lise, some of which results in amusing displays of outrageous guile and stubbornness on Lise's part, a conflict which faintly echoes that between Anne and Nadine in *Les Mandarins*. The events of Lise's life are transposed on to Nadine. Lise at seventeen becomes the mistress of the charming young Spanish Jew Bourla and lives with him, then suffers terrible anguish and loss when he is betrayed to the Gestapo and disappears forever. Nadine's past, although she is just eighteen, includes a similar experience. We are given to understand that at seventeen she had for once known perfect happiness with the gifted young Spaniard Diego, who likewise is tragically betrayed and killed by the Nazis. Nadine's grief over Diego is a component of her unhappiness although its roots go much deeper. Lise befriended the American soldiers in Paris en masse in an insouciant way, mostly scrounging for good meals and cigarettes, but Nadine, suffering from a profound psychological malaise intensified by Diego's death, becomes self-destructive and promiscuous, attempting to "search for Diego from bed to bed." Her parents are disturbed and terrified since she disappears, stays out all night, only to be found dead drunk with a black eye in a seedy bar in Montmartre at dawn. Some episodes are lifted intact from life and put in *Les Mandarins,* such as the luscious banquets dredged up from the black market for the ravenous Lise and her friends by the enterprising Bourla.

In the character of Nadine we have what amounts to a full-fledged case history. Through Anne's reflections on her daughter, the novel provides a psychological explanation of Nadine's provocative and hostile behavior. Nadine is more or less what is technically known as a "rejected" child. Despite Anne's immense kindness and patient good will, she castigates herself for not having loved her daughter with the requisite generous and spontaneous maternal affection. Nadine feels this "rejection" and shows marked hostility to her mother and strenuous competition for her father's affection. It is very redolent of *The Second Sex* as well as standard Freudian material, since the young girls in *The Second Sex* are so often maladjusted and furiously resentful of their mothers. Anne, however, is affection and patience incarnate in comparison with the vengeful and frustrated mothers of *The Second Sex* who maliciously rejoice to see their daughers forced to share their bitter fate. "You too shall be a woman!" Here is Anne's account of Nadine's childhood influences. Anne hasn't been a "good" mother really, but she is not exactly "bad" either:

> I hadn't wanted her; it was Robert who had wanted a child right away. I held a grudge against Nadine for having spoiled the charm of our intimacy. I loved Robert too much and I wasn't egotistical enough to be moved by discovering his features or mine on this little intruder. I observed her blue eyes, hair and nose with scientific detachment. I scolded her as little as possible, but she felt my reserve keenly: she has always been suspicious of me. No little girl ever fought more stubbornly to win her father's affection from her rival, and she has never been resigned to belonging to the same species that I do. [LM, p. 61]

We are instructed about the genesis of Nadine's perplexing unhappiness which takes the form of a disconcerting sexual aggressiveness stemming from her feeling that she is unattractive and unlovable. Nadine's interest in her studies or jobs is erratic. Though she proclaims that she wants to do something interesting, and has some success as an itinerant journalist, accompanying Lambert on news-gathering forays on his motorcycle, she is deterred by her lack of self-confidence. What really matters to her is masculine approval, which she pursues with shameless audacity. Thus work is immediately abandoned in favor of emotional entanglements. In this sense, Nadine is almost a representative case history of *The Second Sex* because, despite her unconventionality and far from docile and passive spirit, she is torn by the question of her femininity, which she seeks to "prove" in very unsatisfactory and agonizing ways.

However, the force and complexity of Nadine's violent and tormented search for self-expression are con-

veyed much more convincingly in her own rampageous
behavior than in Anne's abstract ruminations. Nadine
wants to abandon her studies because she wants to do
"something real." She hates chemistry but has only herself to blame having chosen it not out of ardent interest
but to spite her parents. When her mother placidly suggests that she learn typing so that she can be a secretary
to her father, she quickly drops that project to inform
Anne that at the moment she is simply going off to Portugal with Henri; she has quite literally forced herself on
him. She assumes an insulting and provocative tone with
her mother who, tolerant to a fault, is nonetheless horrified by Nadine's impetuous self-destructiveness. Anne
sensibly points out that Henri is older, attached to another woman and that Nadine will inevitably suffer. Nadine is brutal, cynical and defiant and Anne allows that
she has the right to do what she pleases, but she is aghast
at Nadine's pretense that her relations with Henri or any
man are just a cynical game. Nadine bursts out with a
cruel diatribe full of contempt for her mother and pur-
posely trying to shock her with her brutal frankness
about sex. It is a harrowing scene. Similar verbal battles
between mother and daughter punctuate the novel; Nadine repaying her mother's patience and tolerance with
cruel spitefulness and a perverse desire to shock and
wound. Anne, goaded by Nadine's cynicism, bursts out:

'Scheming, plotting, manipulating, spying on him—you find
that amusing!—and you don't even love him!'
'Maybe I don't love him,' she said, 'but I want him.' She threw
a handful of coals in the grate.
—'With him, I can live, do you understand?'
—'You don't need anyone else in order to live,' I said crossly.
She gazed about her disdainfully: 'You call this living! Frankly,
my poor Mama, do you really think that you've lived? Chatting

with Papa half the day and taking care of crazy people the other half and you call that a *life?''* She got up and dusted off her knees; her voice exasperated me: ''I might do some silly things; I don't say I don't; but I'd rather end up in a brothel than wander through life with stiff kid gloves on: you never take off your gloves. You spend all of your time giving advice; and what do you know about men? And I'm very certain that you never look at yourself in the mirror and that you never have nightmares.' [LM, p. 61]

One often wants to throttle poor Nadine; in this un-called-for attack she hits home and injures Anne far more than she realizes. Nadine is caught in the vicious circle of neurotic personalities who, feeling unloved, wound others and thereby reinforce their original sense of un-worthiness. She certainly shows no signs of that feminine trait so roundly denounced in *The Second Sex* of wanting to *please*. The desire to please according to Simone de Beauvoir is bad because it leads to timidity and insincer-ity. But Nadine's insensitivity to others' feelings and lack of tact are precisely what make her disagreeable.

Nadine's personal relations are always strained. She has the uncanny faculty of ruining even the best moments and spoiling others' natural effervescence and joy in life. She really resents other people's happiness because she herself cannot share it. Her trip to Portugal with Henri is a mournful failure; she relapses into sullen silences or gratuitously annoys Henri by her scorn of him and his work; she hates both the city and the countryside. Indiff-erent to natural beauty, she hotly maintains that the cruel poverty of Portugal spoils it all for her; she inflicts her moral indignation on the natural landscape. Nadine's attitudes are a subtle combination of sincerity and self-deception. She is sincere in her hatred for injustice and indignation at needless suffering; this is demonstrated throughout the novel. Yet her refusal to enjoy the beauty of the sea and the sky with Henri is not really caused by moral indignation at the poverty in Portugal—after all the landscape is not guilty—but rather from her incapacity for simple happiness. As Henri and Nadine leave Lisbon they have an unpleasant experience at a "pâtisserie" where they are accosted by two pathetic little wretches who beg for some of the pastry Nadine has bought; Henri tells Nadine what they have said, which is heartrending. They said: "How lucky you are to be able to eat when you're hungry." Nadine is violently upset and weeps in the car as they leave. She gains our sympathy because she does have the power to be genuinely moved by others' suffering. Yet her unhappiness and her tears are also tears for herself if not really for herself alone; one has the impression that this overwrought reaction is triggered by her own malaise and desolate sense of the sadness of all things.

Nadine's furious absolutism, so characteristic of Beauvoirian heroines, is also shot through with dishonesty and bad faith. She is a living replica of the young girl of *The Second Sex* who dreams of perfection but who has never risked anything. Her moral superiority is fraudulent. Nadine's essential frivolity is painfully apparent but rather amusing. In so many of her morally exigent feminine characters (Paule, Xavière, Régine, et al.) Simone de Beauvoir gives us almost a parody of her own absolutist, all-or-nothing temperament. They are in a way absurd caricatures of "l'homme révolté," but after all they are only women. Nadine exudes scorn for Henri's hosts, some left-wing politicians in Portugal: "Your old gentlemen with starched collars; they'd look very fine behind the glass cases at the Musée de l'Homme, but as revolutionaries, don't make me laugh." "*I find them moving," Henri said. "And you know they take enormous risks." "They talk a lot." She let sand dribble between her fingers. "Words, as the good man says, just words." (LM, p. 92) She herself has a brilliant solution: "Instead of talking so much, I would bring down Salazar with one good rifle shot." She has the same standard of negative perfectionism about *any* human activity. She scorns Henri's writing because he cannot be sure he is a genius. Henri's excellent defense of his métier simply provokes Nadine's habitual "sulky voice." Much of Nadine's absolutism is really a profound negativism which stems from her own lack of self-esteem so that her arguments are all tinged with envy and spite. Incapable of the élan and commitment that other people have, she takes refuge in her superior world of absolute negation.

The characters of *Les Mandarins* do a prodigious amount of mere talking, but there are occasionally some scenes of exciting violence, usually fomented by Nadine. She almost slaps a woman journalist in the face for "spying" on the Dubreuilh's; she peremptorily dashes off to Paris while the others discuss the intrigues and cabals of their literary and political enemies and, breathlessly returning while her family is still at the table, announces proudly that she cooly walked into Lambert's office and whacked him hard on the face for having written derogatory remarks about Henri's book. She is now a wife and mother, but undeterred by her new-found adult dignity. The book ends with a harrowing episode in which one of Robert's old companions, Sézenac, arrives in a desperate state at the Dubreuilh's house in the country, fleeing from his pursuers who had discovered that, a drug addict, he had *sold* Jews by the thousands to the Nazis during the war to obtain money for his drugs. Henri, Anne, and Robert are sickened and horrified but lack the heart for vengeance three years after the war, and regard Sézenac as a pitiful human derelict. But Nadine, outraged, cries out for revenge and secretly telephones Vincent, who races out to the house and shoots Sézenac. Later she sobs with remorse. Her violence is provoked by real moral indignation, but is futile and hysterical.

Nadine's spiritual malaise is intimately bound up with her feelings about her femininity which she attempts to prove by violent sexual agressiveness; at the same time she resents her feminine condition and often uses it as an excuse for her inadequacies, just as though she had read *The Second Sex.* She is a classic case of a tortured feminine being, torn because she wants to be feminine, loved and admired by men, and yet violent and aggressive and defiantly insisting that soft and gentle femininity is not for her. Her case is one only a professional could untangle, but seems to demonstrate that one's femininity or one's happy acceptance of it are intrinsically connected with a person's whole psychic equilibrium so that one's attitude toward one's sexual role and toward one's self are inextricably bound up together. By deft and persistent little concrete strokes the author conveys the pathos of Nadine's not quite successful "feminine" enterprise. Henri observes Nadine: "She became almost pretty when she smiled; but her face splotched with little red marks stayed impassive; he said to himself, 'Poor Nadine.' " (LM, p. 93) Nadine returning from Portugal with some new finery compels masculine admiration: "A real lady, eh?" said Nadine turning on her heels; with her fur coat, stockings and her pumps she had an elegant and almost feminine look." (LM, p. 96) Or: "She had tried to put on makeup artfully, but her lashes looked like the prickles of a sea-urchin and she had black smudges under her eyes." (LM, p. 123) Nadine is pathetic but fetching in her ineptitude in the womanly arts. At any rate her clumsiness is more appealing than the horrible calculated elegance and perfection as "objects" of Elizabeth and the "femmes du monde." A profoundly impaired self-esteem is the key to Nadine's equivocal feelings about her femininity.

Nadine constantly denigrates her feminine state and admires and envies men extravagantly; she exalts men in a way they scarcely deserve and demands impossible wonders of them who are after all only human beings like herself, not gods. In this way Nadine is also a living demonstration of *The Second Sex* where women are inclined in general to regard masculinity as enviable and awesome. Although Nadine and Lambert become lovers and she appears at times vaguely happy, she ultimately destroys their rapport by her rancor and contempt for Lambert, in whom she cannot forgive a single weakness or transgression. She regards his kindness to his own father, suspected of handing over Jews during the war, as an iniquitous and unpardonable crime. The wrangling and mutual harrassment between Nadine and Lambert attains inspired paroxysms of pointless destructiveness, but Nadine is always the instigator of these scenes, which she seems in a way to enjoy. Their final rupture occurs in a confrontation of stupefying violence when Lambert rushes to the scene of Nadine's accident on his much envied motorcycle which she has stolen in a rage; he slaps her out of sheer exasperation at the worry and pain she has caused them all. Whereupon she erupts in a frenzy of self-pity and rage, shrieking that he cares more for his motorcycle than her, and hurls unjust taunts at him until he leaves, stunned by the enormity of her violent invective. She even accuses him of complicity in the death of his mistress Rosa who—Nadine insinuates—was knowingly handed over to the Gestapo by Lambert's father. It is an appalling scene, but one can feel how Nadine's unforgivable behavior is propelled by her pathetic belief that no one can really love her, which in turn engenders a fanatical injured pride and violent defensiveness. All the thorny prickliness of neurotic personalities who take offense at the least injury and react with violence to imagined slights reaches an apogee in Nadine. As she says to Henri, "I have been mistrustful since the day I was born."

Nadine's despair is so individual that it transcends easy explanation purely in terms of her feminine condition; it seems more a component of her forlorn rejected-child mentality. A conversation between Anne and Nadine reveals the depths of her self-hatred. It is characteristically studded with Nadine's unladylike vocabulary so in keeping with her constant attitude of defiance. She has miraculously passed her exams but this means nothing to her. She undermines herself in this way:

'It's all the same thing whether I flunk or pass. I'll never make a career out of chemistry.' She thought it over a minute. 'I can't have a career in anything. I'n not an intellectual and when it comes to action I don't have any guts. I'm not useful for anything. She shook her head: "I suppose that at bottom I'm really made to have a husband and children like all women. I'll scour my pots and produce a sniveling brat every year.'
—'If you marry just to marry, you won't be happy either.'
—'Oh, don't worry! No man will be dumb enough to marry me. They like to sleep with me but after that—goodbye. I'm not attractive to men.' [LM, p. 201]

Anne who understands Nadine's complicated strategies of self-derision and defiance kindly insists that Lambert is very fond of Nadine and has had eyes for no one else for a whole year. Whereupon Nadine explains that Lambert must be a pederast! No *man* could love her apparently. Besides she adds she doesn't care anyway since she doesn't fancy becoming merely the replacement for Rosa, "a substitute product." It is all infinitely pathetic. She wistfully envies Lambert's golden opportunity to wander adventurously through France on a motorcycle—just like Colonel Lawrence, an allusion that recalls an exact passage in *The Second Sex* where Simone de Beauvoir laments that women are not permitted to live the kind of swashbuckling and daring life of a T. E. Lawrence —so essential for a writer. Nadine is demonstrably the reflection of Simone de Beauvoir's long cogitations on the woman question *(Les Mandarins* follows *The Second Sex).* Her sad, envious, and rancorous self-lacerating defiance express more poignantly than any generalization the disadvantage of being female.

Yet Nadine as a splendidly realized fictional character also casts doubt on the dogmatic assertions of *The Second Sex.* So often *The Second Sex* in its extreme emphasis on woman's woes seems to imply that the female sex en masse is uniquely prone to neurosis, inner division, and unsalubrious character traits because of the thankless cultural and biological role imposed on it by a masculine-dominated society. In speaking of young girls, for example, Simone de Beauvoir likens their behavior to neurotic behavior. Indeed Nadine actually *is* a neurotic personality. But is she neurotic just because she is female? The carefully plotted explanations of Nadine by Anne have a distinctly Freudian flavor. Since Nadine has grown up in a radically liberated atmosphere where the traditional stereotypes and oppressive "feminine" upbringing should not have had their malign effects, it would be reasonable to conclude that her tormented conflicts about herself and her femininity are more a result of individual psychology than of the oppressive and discouraging environment all feminine beings must submit to. On the question of "femininity" *The Second Sex* is very perplexing when one considers a real example like Nadine. Simone de Beauvoir says Nadine succeeds "neither in becoming feminine nor in transcending her femininity." "Becoming feminine" is often regarded by Simone de Beauvoir as something suspect or limiting, a kind of "surrender." And yet Nadine's misery is so extreme; it is not clear how she can conceivably "transcend" her femininity nor why she would even want to. No one wants to be sexless; so it would appear that accepting and even enjoying one's own natural condition is fundamental. "Femininity" in Nadine's case appears to be a profoundly real entity and not just some bogus myth engendered by a heartless and blind masculine culture. With Nadine it is not a question of being "la vraie femme" according to the reactionary views of Simone de Beauvoir's father, but rather simply of being a woman, or even just a reasonably contented *person.* Simone de Beauvoir often appears to feel that one can "become feminine" or not at will, which is debatable.

The Second Sex is really not altogether clear about what "femininity" is. When Simone de Beauvoir actually creates a sad character like Nadine, whose tragic division is highly convincing, the fiendish complexity of the conception of "femininity" and all its ramifications is manifest: some of the dogmatic and simplistic assertions of *The Second Sex* seem then unequal to the infinite complexity of human character and situation. As has often been noted, the theoretical certainties are sometimes modified or contradicted by the imponderable human complexities which appear in the richer and more ambiguous world of Simone de Beauvoir's fiction. At the same time, the melancholy thesis of *The Second Sex* that feminine creatures are peculiarly prone to suffer is constantly reinforced by the feminine characters of the novels. Xavière to some extent, unhappy and ineffectual, and Nadine especially, in all her plaintive violence, are worthy specimens of Beauvoirian afflicted femininity. When reproached for never having depicted a single really "emancipated" woman who would personify her ideal, Simone de Beauvoir replied as previously cited that she painted women primarily as she sees them, "divided." Nowhere is a "positive" heroine to be found. In this Simone de Beauvoir is perfectly consistent and true to her own convictions: her feminine characters in spite of their diversity reflect with faultless precision her fundamental pessimism about the feminine condition. In *Les Mandarins* a woman appears for only a second, a supernumerary with no status as a character whatsoever, and she is disposed of in one sentence, but what a characteristic Beauvoirian sentence! "I watched Samazelle from the corner of my eye; he didn't seem at all embarrassed; his wife had a tortured look; but she always looked like that."

NOTES

1. In *The Second Sex,* in a brilliant analysis of Stendhal's "myth" about women Simone de Beauvoir does however give his heroines their due. She recognizes their charm and force of character, and in so doing indicates that her theory is somewhat one-sided and simplistic. Stendhal's heroines are members of an oppressed class and are the "inessential" as far as the world goes, but they are superior human beings and embody everything that Stendhal admires. Stendhal's values are *not,* however, the world's, while Simone de Beauvoir's *are* in the last analysis (success, power, fame, money, action, etc.).

2. It must be said that today American women who are bravely carrying the torch for Simone de Beauvoir's brand of feminism do indeed have a "challenging" attitude toward men. They realize at last that woman's full equality is not a matter of individual salvation but a real class conflict, and only by challenging the male establishment politically, legally, intellectually, economically and socially is there any hope for general emancipation. The old-fashioned subtlety of male oppression through insidious forms of male chauvinism has been rigorously dissected. We now see that women cannot have it both ways and expect to win equality. You cannot flatter and ingratiate yourself with the male establishment and expect to get wholesale acceptance. Men have always counted on subtle intimidation to keep woman in her place. (She's not "feminine," she's "challenging.") The mere subject of unjust treatment of women used to be and still is taboo in some quarters because it offends male sensibilities! I'm afraid Simone de Beauvoir is being a little unfair to the sisterhood here and evinces certain attitudes typical of the "token" woman who has "made it." I am astonished she could never have felt "male chauvinism," but maybe Frenchmen are different from American men.

3. Even the real Olga, like Xavière, sometimes resented the invention of a mythical Olga when she preferred her own humble human reality. The eighteen-year-old Olga responded negatively to the reluctantly aging thirty-year-old Sartre's and Beauvoir's cult of youth and their habit of turning her into a symbolic marvel: "She claimed to ignore the humiliating limitations of the human condition which we couldn't resign ourselves entirely to either; therefore we liked to attribute wondrous symbolic values to her. She became Rimbaud, Antigone, "les enfants terribles," a dark angel who judged us from the heights of her sparkling heaven. She did nothing herself to promote this metamorphosis; on the contrary, she was quite annoyed with it; she detested the supernatural character who had usurped her place." (LFDL'A, p. 279)

4. It is true, however, that much of Xavière's charm emanates from her youth and freshness—a sort of "beauté du diable" quality that is intrinsic to youth. Certainly in terms of *The Second Sex,* Xavière would appear to be a good candidate for the role of the woman who wakes up one fine morning to find her beauty and charm gone and nothing else to sustain her. *The Second Sex's* message that women cannot expect to depend on *charm* to see them through is incontestable.

5. (*L'Invitée,* p. 443) In this respect, Xavière is almost a "positive" heroine by *The Second Sex* standards. Her scorn of "devoted love" and altruism echoes the author's own attitudes towards the traditional "good" woman. In this episode, though, she is shown to be egotistical and hateful while Françoise, whose values she mocks, is more admirable. The ambiguities involved in any simplistic theory about altruism versus enlightened self-interest show up here.

6. Aury, p. 326.

6

Simone de Beauvoir on Motherhood
and "Le Dévouement"

Whereas many aspects of Simone de Beauvoir's theory about women are standard feminist doctrine, her concept of motherhood and her denigration of this part of woman's destiny are so extreme that most critics are obliged to demur. Geneviève Gennari, who admires Simone de Beauvoir's work and subscribes in toto to most of *The Second Sex,* notes the pessimistic implications of the book, since motherhood, which *is* woman's biological destiny, is regarded as an impediment to self-fulfillment. She says: "Certainly Simone de Beauvoir is unacquainted with the very simple but deep love which is experienced between mother and child in the vast majority of cases."[1] Mlle. Gennari suspects that this pessimism manifested in "the underlying refusal of the entire book to grant maternity the important place it has in the life of a woman," is not just the revolt of a superior woman against woman's maternal role but part of the revolt of existentialist philosophy against the absurdity of a life which is content to repeat itself. She explains the "existentialist" side of Simone de Beauvoir's feelings about human reproduction: "When Simone de Beauvoir in *The Second Sex* confesses her aversion to the mysterious turmoil in the fetus—'this quivering gelatine which is wrought in the womb'—alluding to it as the 'sluggish stickiness of carrion,' she does it as a philosopher and the 'slimy stickiness' is not reserved for the anatomy of interior female organs; it is identified with existential nausea whose horror men also know.''[2] Precisely. Simone de Beauvoir's entire philosophy is reflected in *Le Deuxième Sexe* where woman's immanence, passivity, and essential entrapment by her biological destiny are the initial source of her malediction. According to Simone de Beauvoir's existentialist criteria these are fundamental evils. A quarrel with *The Second Sex* is also a quarrel with Simone de Beauvoir's brand of existentialism. *The Second Sex* never really settles the question whether woman's malediction is imposed from without or is intrinsic, but the attitude toward motherhood makes it seem intrinsic. Still Simone de Beauvoir also insists that woman is not born but made; it is sheer cultural conditioning that tranforms her into the "second sex."

The maternal enterprise is metaphysically and ethically suspect, and despite an occasional admission that some women apparently find motherhood rewarding, the vast weight of the evidence plus the negative and derogatory tone which informs the author's prose, convey a most dismal impression of this not inconsiderable feminine role. Woman as mother is a passive instrument, prey to the species, etc., etc. After two volumes this distinction becomes tediously familiar. The following passage is typical: woman's biological destiny is somehow a natural disaster because her freedom is compromised by having to reproduce: "The transcendence of the artisan, of the man of action, contains the element of subjectivity; but in the mother-to-be the antithesis of subject and object ceases to exist; she and the child with which she is swollen make up together an equivocal pair overwhelmed by life.

Ensnared by nature, the pregnant woman is plant and animal, a stockpile of colloids, an incubator, an egg; she scares children proud of their young, straight bodies and makes young people titter contemptuously because she is a human being, a conscious and free individual, who has become life's passive instrument." (TSS, II, p. 467) This is the standard approach and the horrors of childbirth are demonstrated with countless cases including that of the reliable Sophie Tolstoy, an inexhaustible mine of pertinent illustration of all the dolorous themes of the book. Naturally childbirth joins the list of Sophie's feminine complaints: "These nine months have been the most terrible of my life. As for the tenth, it's better not to speak of it." (TSS, II, p. 480) Not that there is any particular merit in simply bearing a child, at least according to logic, but Simone de Beauvoir employs existentialist rhetoric to destroy any natural, instinctual satisfaction that women might take from this accomplishment. She habitually uses abstract reasoning to prove the fallaciousness of natural feelings.

Simone de Beauvoir appears at times to be merely battling against the traditional sanctification of motherhood and the sentimental nonsense that maternity should be woman's crowning glory and sole achievement: woman's natural functions are her sole raison d'être. This is the venerable argument of male imperialists like Norman Mailer; men never seem to tire of this ancient platitude and it is actually still, mirabile dictu, used as a legitimate argument to deny women equal rights. If a woman is a mother, she cannot be anything else: except of course household drudge, waitress, shop girl, typist, clerk, nurse, school teacher, secretary, or dental assistant. But motherhood shuts her out from the higher spheres where money, power, and prestige reign. But Simone de Beauvoir is not just exposing the use of motherhood to "keep woman in her place." She has a distinct bias against it. She usually implies that both the having of children and raising them belong in the category of immanence and passivity and are thus inferior, second-rate activities. As she says, mothers don't *do* anything. Her attitude is very depressing and one often gets the impression that motherhood for her consists of the mere production of children by maladjusted mothers who perpetrate without end their own character defects. ("and this long chain of misery perpetuates itself indefinitely").[3] Occasionally Simone de Beauvoir has to recognize the positive side of parenthood which common sense compels us to regard as an important activity since children are after all the raw material of the future. At one point she admits that having children is "un engagement" since it clearly involves moral choice and commitment. Here Simone de Beauvoir gives the standard feminist argument and she is eloquent. It is precisely *because* women are the mothers of the race that they should be treated decently! She exposes the ancient hypocrisy of exalting motherhood while at the same time reducing its practictioners to the status of second-class citizen:

"There is an extravagant fraudulence in the easy reconciliation made between the common attitude of contempt for women and the respect shown for mothers. It is outrageously paradoxical to deny women all activity in public affairs, to shut her out of masculine careers, to assert her incapacity in all fields of effort, and then to entrust to her the most delicate and the most serious undertaking of all: the molding of a human being." (TSS, II, p. 494) However, for the most part, *Le Deuxième Sexe* actually indicts motherhood, maintaining that it is a vicarious way of living and not therefore authentic. A mother lives for and through another and not for herself.

Self-fulfillment means just that, and serving other people cannot lead to it, no matter what saints and do-gooders might say to the contrary.

In addition, *The Second Sex* swarms with forbidding and frightening mothers. Motherhood brings out the worst in women, no mistake. Either they are sadistic, capricious, or dominating or else they take the opposite tack and oppress their children by their masochistic devotion. The reason for the general malignancy in mothers is that they feel they have been betrayed: motherhood has been held out as the golden goal of "feminine" self-fulfillment but they discover it is an enormous fraud. Not finding self-fulfillment, they take revenge on their children. No one would deny that the world abounds with terrible mothers, but *The Second Sex* darkly assumes that the condition itself is responsible; it is so intrinsically unrewarding that it generates boredom, resentment, martyrdom and masochism. This is a fine antidote to traditional sentimental effusions about hallowed motherhood, but the picture is so one-sided that it distorts reality. Even a mother's taking her baby to the public garden is somehow reprehensible ("an alibi"), and the gaiety and charm of young children are a miserably small compensation for the endless care and chagrin they entail. The tone is implacable; the emotional rewards of motherhood elude Simone de Beauvoir. According to her, mothers are almost always incapable of regarding their children as free, autonomous human beings, to be appreciated and loved for their own sake. Children are rather the means through which the mother finds emotional satisfaction of one kind or another, often of a perverse sort. Mothers do not have a fine grasp of Kantian ethics or neo-freudian psychology or any enlightened and humane conception of human conduct.

The Second Sex presents a series of little tableaux of

family life in which the various members of this accursed gathering exhibit nothing but morosity, boredom, contempt, hostility and total incomprehension. About the following family scene one can't help wondering if such people would be gloriously redeemed if they were immured in an orphanage or alone in a boarding house or a hotel. Is it the abominable institution of the family or their own unimaginative mediocrity that weighs upon them? Here is the family:

> He (the husband) is in no hurry to get home, dreading the all too frequent scene in which she takes a small revenge for her boredom and expresses her anticipated disappointment in an appearance hardly worth waiting for. And the husband is disappointed, too, even if she keeps silence on her wrongs. He is tired from his work and has a contradictory desire for rest and stimulation, which she fails to satisfy. [Nor do the children provide entertainment or peace; the dinner and evening are endured with vague ill-humor.] The evening is dull: reading, radio, desultory talks; each remains alone under cover of this intimacy. The wife wonders, with hope or apprehension, whether tonight—at last—"something will happen." [TSS, II, p. 448]

Simone de Beauvoir's animus against motherhood is both metaphysical and ethical and in accordance with her entire system of values. The traditional praise of the womanly virtues is derived from the maternal role which the masculine culture has always somewhat hypocritically exalted. Simone de Beauvoir rejects these virtues as being either vastly exaggerated or illusory or even faults masquerading as virtues. The classic elevation of motherhood has always heaped encomiums on the disinterested devotion of mother love which gives all, suffers, and asks nothing in return. Although Simone de Beauvoir regards generosity as one of the highest human qualities, the kind of generosity that motherhood involves does not fire her imagination. *The Second Sex* is in fact almost a tract against "le dévouement", a traditional ingredient of mother love. ("Le dévouement" can either mean "devotion," "attachment," or "self-sacrifice". The third meaning of course makes it sound masochistic and martyrlike. I use the French term to express simply what we mean in ordinary language by "mother love", but of course Simone de Beauvoir wants to stress the unhealthy "self-sacrifice" part of it.) Subjected to a continuous barrage of propaganda, women are encouraged and exhorted to fulfill themselves in the most "womanly" way possible, by devoting themselves to others. Women are in effect the Christian martyrs of human society, not by choice but by indoctrination. Since involuntary martyrdom is not really conducive to the finest human development, but generates resentment and subtle forms of tyranny and revenge, women who accept this fate become warped, embittered, and limited human beings. Simone de Beauvoir's philosophy emphasizes the unlimited freedom of each person, the ideal of self-development through work; human worth is measured exclusively in terms of what one *does*. But mothers do not do anything, according to Simone de Beauvoir's definition. Egoism in the sense of individual self-enhancement is admirable; altruism in the sense of living for others is a kind of self-mutilation. Therefore the traditional virtues of "le dévouement" are injurious to the self and cannot lead to self-fulfillment. Simone de Beauvoir's critique of the false snares of "le dévouement" is very penetrating and her bias against altruism has a very Nietszchean ring. The traditional view, always the whipping dog of her arguments, that marriage and children should be woman's sole occupation and "fulfillment" is attacked by Simone de Beauvoir, who rightly questions the assumption that the feminine portion of the human race should somehow be regarded as without egoism and perfectly content to receive all its satisfaction in life from simply serving others.

In *Pyrrhus et Cinéas,* a philosophical essay, Simone de Beauvoir analyses the concept of "le dévouement" and concludes that it is both undesirable and impossible. Her arguments are based on the premise that "le dévouement" is something total and all-embracing. She assumes that "le dévouement" means a total renouncement of egoism: motherhood for example is pure self-sacrifice. "Because devotion first appears as total resignation in favor of another person." (P et C, p. 310) With this as a premise all the rest follows. What she gives us is really a devastating exposure of false familial affection. "Le dévouement" is always suspect because it seeks a reward in the form of gratitude, dependence of the other, etc. She shows the difficulty of determining anyone else's good. By her definition Simone de Beauvoir makes "le dévouement" something inherently sinister, an infringement on another's freedom, because it implies that one person will decide another's good, which is presumptuous and impossible. Here is her argument why "le dévouement" is impossible:

> Our actions should be directed by lucid generosity. We should be responsible for our own choices and we should have as ends situations which will be a starting point for others. But we should not entertain the delusion that we can do anything for another. This is what our examination of devoted love teaches us: its claims cannot be justified; the end which it envisages is impossible. Not only can we not abdicate our own freedom in favor of another person nor ever act completely in another's behalf, but we cannot do anything for anyone else. This is because there is no stable, unmoving state of being happy

which is in our power to grant the other person, there is no
paradise for him to enter whose key is in our hands; his real
good is that freedom which belongs only to him and which
carries him far beyond every possible gift; this good is forever
outside of our reach. [P et C, p. 325]

This argument seems clearly false. Naturally one cannot
guarantee another's happiness or create a paradise for
him to enter, etc. But that does not mean the "le dévouement" is impossible or necessarily a false kind of
generosity. Why cannot it be generous?[4] Simone de
Beauvoir describes in *Pyrrhus et Cinéas* the good kind of
parental affection which does not regard the child as an
object, a possession, or a source of undying obedience
and gratitude. Why cannot "le dévouement" fit this conception? What difference does it make what one calls it?
It is not parental affection as such which is not generous
but rather the perverted and misguided forms of it. But
to say one cannot do *anything* for another person or that
because children ultimately leave and transcend their
parents' gifts, the parent has not really *given* anything
appears sophistical. The chances of a child's present and
future happiness would appear to be somewhat greater
if he has a warm and generous mother than if he grows
up in an orphange or in a den of thieves. And one might
conclude that this mother had given him something, in-
tangible as the gift is.

Simone de Beauvoir's bias against altruism and "le
dévouement" are part of her bias against motherhood;
any limitation of individual freedom is undesirable according to her ethics, although it is not clear how
generosity naturally flows from unbridled freedom. In
The Second Sex the values which are continually extolled
and admired are ambition, self-fulfillment, power, action

—fundamentally egoistic values; this partly accounts for Simone de Beauvoir's depreciation of "le dévouement." There is very little recognition of the fact that some sort of compromise or delicate balance between egoism and altruism is essential if love or generosity or real human affection can even exist. At any rate the traditional virtues of motherhood appear pale and vapid in Simone de Beauvoir's eyes; maternal generosity is transmuted into "le dévouement", an equivocal and suspect substitute for real generosity.[5] Motherhood can never lead to "la gloire" and all of Simone de Beauvoir's philosophical arguments and emotional bias against motherhood reflect a fundamental distaste for the classic feminine virtues which do not include power, success, and changing the face of the world in the sublime masculine manner.[5]

How is one to explain this aversion to motherhood so pronounced in Simone de Beauvoir's writings? *Mémoires d'Une Jeune Fille Rangée* provides ample clues. Simone de Beauvoir's energetic and sanguine temperament, never docile and passive even as a child, plus the general lugubrious feminine atmosphere of her own family and class did not help to instill a desire for motherhood in her. Her childhood was happy and being a girl was a natural and joyous part of her existence which she savored to the full. However, she recounts that in her childish games with dolls she used to like to play being a nurse who gathered up the wounded on the battlefield, but didn't take care of them later, which was dull. Or, when she and her sister played house it is always responsibility and power, not tedious domesticity which interests her. Their husbands would be conveniently absent so they could run the show: "But I refused to let a man deprive me of my rightful responsibilities; our husbands would travel. I knew very well that in life things were quite different: the mother of the family is always under the surveillance of her husband; a thousand thankless tasks weigh her down. When I imagined my future I regarded this state of servitude as so onerous that I balked at the prospect of having children; what mattered to me was moulding minds and characters: I decided to be a teacher." (MD'UJFR, p. 56)

Everything about Simone de Beauvoir even as a child expressed a fiercely striving temperament and it is not surprising that the lack of "éclat" in the maternal role should have failed to elicit her enthusiasm. *Mémoires d'Une Jeune Fille Rangée* resounds with vague dreams of grandeur and accomplishment. Simone de Beauvoir had a mania for activity. In a way her philosophy reflects her middle-class upbringing because it celebrates action and accomplishment, which she learned to appreciate early. Even as a child she was a "doer." She recounts: "Can't this child stay still a minute without doing anything," my uncle Maurice asked impatiently; my parents laughed at this as much as I did; they disapproved of idleness. I thought idleness all the more reprehensible because it bored me. That's the reason that my life was so happy during this period; I only had to follow my natural bent and everyone was enchanted with me." (MD'UJFR, p. 65) Simone de Beauvoir never yearns for calm domestic tranquility; even when she dreams of an imaginary husband who will "subjugate" her by his superlative intellect she concludes: "Life in common would have to promote, not thwart, my basic ambition; that is, to be the master of my own destiny." (MD'UJFR, p. 140)

The feminine sphere in Simone de Beauvoir's family and class was not inspiring: the women were generally less well-educated than their husbands, deferent to their opinions, pious and conventional, and their domestic "corvées" were horrendously taxing. Even with ample domestic help they managed to give the impression of being weighed down with heavy and solemn responsibilities. Simone de Beauvoir was no doubt furnished priceless material for *The Second Sex* in some of these family portraits. Aunt Hélène is a superb example of futile feminine martyrdom: "Aunt Hélène used to inspect her closets starting at six in the morning. She had an ample supply of domestic servants so that she did none of the housework, cooked rarely, never read and never sewed, and yet she would complain that she never had a minute to herself: she would relentlessly rummage about the house from attic to cellar with fierce concentration." (MD'UJFR, p. 75) The epic boredom and vegetative mindlessness that enveloped Aunt Hélène's family of country squires is delightfully evoked by Simone de Beauvoir. These family vignettes often surpass *The Second Sex* in their picturesque rendition of the defects of family life. The middle-class women in Simone de Beauvoir's childhood delighted in orgies of excessive domestic preparation and ceremony; relatives were always coming to tea and tea was not a light affair. Simone de Beauvoir's description of the domestic servitude of her friend Zaza is harrowing: "Domestic chores consumed her mornings. They would gather flowers, arrange bouquets and above all, they would cook. Lili, Zaza, and Babelle would concoct little cakes, quatre-quarts, biscuits and brioches for the afternoon tea. They helped their mother and grandmother can tons of fruits and vegetables; there were always peas to shell, beans to snap, nuts to shell and prunes to pit. Feeding the family became an exhausting task which required generous slices of [female] time and labor." (MD'UJFR, p. 244) The whole feminine world seemed dreadfully limited and unexciting; Simone de Beauvoir's description of her contemporaries at le Cours

Désir passively awaiting arranged marriages and drab future domesticity is mournful. To paraphrase Wordsworth: "Shades of the prison house close in upon the growing girl." Her father is not impressed with her schoolmates in spite of his enthusiasm for "la vraie femme." "What must have especially struck my father was the dejected and crushed expression of these adolescent girls." Simone de Beauvoir sees them again after having tasted the heady delights of the Sorbonne and the cleavage is total: . . . "I continued to go forward, I kept on developing my talents while they, in order to adjust to their role of marriagable girls, began to get duller and duller." (MD'UJFR, p. 168)

The character of Simone de Beauvoir's mother without doubt contributed to her rejection of the feminine vocation. Her portrait is sympathetic but detached and Simone de Beauvoir admits that she admired her father much more. Her mother was not someone she wished to resemble; she displays many rather sad limitations that women in *The Second Sex* so often have: lacking self-assurance and exuberance she compensates for this by a rigid moralism, dominating spirit and an implacable faith in the conventions. Simone de Beauvoir pictures her as both pathetic and formidable:

> Her childhood and youth had afflicted her with feelings of resentment that never entirely left her. At twenty, looking stiff in her 'guimpe à baleine' [whaleboned skirt?], trained to repress her enthusiasm and to bury her bitter secrets in silence, she felt lonely and misunderstood: in spite of her beauty, she lacked gaiety and self-assurance.
>
> . . . In her eyes my father possessed enormous prestige and she thought that women should obey and look up to men. But with Louise, my sister, and me she proved to be very authoritarian and sometimes this led to passionate outbursts when her will

was thwarted. If one of her intimate friends or a member of the family annoyed her or injured her feelings, she often reacted angrily and would be ruthlessly frank and cutting. . . . When she felt unthreatened, however, she was always timid. . . . Her youth, her inexperience, her love for my father made her vulnerable; she dreaded criticism, and to avoid it, she took great pains to be just like everybody else. [MD'UJFR, p. 38]

Simone de Beauvoir's mother was deeply religious and represents a fine example of "le dévouement"; but her ideas were utterly conventional and she meekly accepted all the *idées reçues* of her husband about politics and the innate moral superiority of the middle class. As a young child Simone de Beauvoir enjoyed her mother's affection, but she lacked the kind of prestige and imposing presence to make her daughter wish to emulate her. "Her behavior complied with her beliefs; quick to sacrifice herself, she devoted herself entirely to her family." (MD'UJFR, p. 40)

Thus as there are no examples in Simone de Beauvoir's fiction of her ideal "emancipated" woman, except Anne and Françoise, who fall short because they lack self-assertiveness, so there are no characters who represent the traditional "womanly" woman—There is no one who actually embodies those traits admired in maternity—generosity, compassion and warmth. Anne and Françoise both have these qualities to some extent, but they are regarded as being in some way a deterrent to their full self-realization. Anne is too docile and devoted to her family according to Simone de Beauvoir, although she partly fails at motherhood too by her own account. Françoise is outgoing and generous, a model of "les amours de dévouement" according to the scornful Xavière, but she feels that these very qualities in herself somehow make her weak and dependent. She lacks "being." But in *Mémoires d'Une Jeune Fille Rangée* there is a memorable and touching portrait of Simone de Beauvoir's childhood friend Zaza who, in my opinion, epitomizes in many aspects these traditional feminine qualities. Next to Simone de Beauvoir she is the most vivid person in the book. The author's portrayal of her death is exceptionally moving for she manages to create the feeling that Zaza's death was unnecessary; she is a tragic victim of the imbecility and false moral pretensions of her bourgeois family. Although she dies from a disease, Simone de Beauvoir's artistry is so accomplished that we accept her verdict and we feel outrage that the enchanting Zaza had to die a martyr to middle-class morality.

Of course Zaza is shown as a child and dies young and so she is amorphous and changing and must remain as mostly potentiality; yet she lived to be twenty years old and exhibits a forceful individuality and pronounced character which compelled Simone de Beauvoir's admiration and affection. At the age of ten Simone and Zaza became fast friends; they are called "les deux inséparables." They share the same tastes for reading and study but Zaza dazzles Simone de Beauvoir by her originality and audacity; the independence and daring of Zaza seem particularly remarkable since Simone de Beauvoir feels that she herself lacks "personality." She recounts: "Suddenly she seemed to me to be somebody. The way she talked to the teachers amazed me; her naturalness made a startling contrast with the stereotyped voices of the other pupils. The following week she finally won me over completely; she mimicked Mlle. Bolet with marvelous precision; everything she said seemed interesting or droll." (MDJFR, p. 87) Once during a piano recital Zaza behaves with a daring which "bordered on scandal."

Decked out in her taffeta dress she plays a piece which her mother had deemed too difficult but she acquits herself splendidly: "This time she performed the piece faultlessly, and casting a triomphant look at Madame Mabille she stuck out her tongue at her mother. The little girls trembled beneath their curls and the young ladies' faces froze with disapproval. When Zaza came down off the platform her mother hugged her so happily that no one dared to scold her. In my eyes this escapade crowned her with glory. Submissive to the rules, to conventions, to prejudice, I nevertheless loved what was youthful, spontaneous and sincere. Zaza's vivacity and independence captivated me." (MDJFR, p. 89)

Zaza is intelligent and sensitive but furthermore she has an independence of spirit and the courage of her own convictions that awe Simone de Beauvoir. She even has good taste; she dares to mock accepted opinion and prim respectability. Simone de Beauvoir describes how the two friends were different:

> Enthusiastic and uncritical, I was interested in everything: Zaza was selective: Greece enchanted her, the Romans bored her; indifferent to the misfortunes of the royal family, she was enraptured with Napoleon. She admired Racine, but Corneille irritated her; she detested *Horace* and *Polyeucte* but *Le Misanthrope* ignited her great fellow-feeling. I had always observed her mocking spirit; between the ages of twelve and fifteen she adopted irony as a mode of behavior; she ridiculed not only most people but also established customs and received ideas; she made La Rochefoucauld's *Maximes* her bedside reading and would repeat at every turn that men are ruled by self-interest. [MDJFR, p. 109]

Simone de Beauvoir particularly admired what she called Zaza's "cynisme"; what she means is that Zaza belonged to the pure-in-heart who know what is really good and her cynicism is a mask for her disdain for the hypocritical facsimile of the real thing she saw about her. Zaza can penetrate the hypocrisy of her milieu: "In their circle they talked a lot about God, charity, and the ideal; but Zaza was quick to notice that her relatives only respected money, social position, and respectability. This hypocrisy revolted her; she protected herself from it by affecting the guise of cynicism. I never noticed then the heart-breaking and grating tone in what they used to call her "paradoxes" at the Cours Désir." (MDJFR, p. 114) Zaza is at heart the antithesis of cynicism: she is warm-hearted, generous, and has passionate convictions. Her genuine capacity for sympathy and out-going concern for others is apparent throughout her whole history. Though sharp-witted and caustic, she is extremely sensitive. Zaza adores children and it astonished Simone de Beauvoir that she could "get ecstatic about rumple-faced newborn babies." Simone and Zaza disagree on the subject of motherhood. Zaza thinks having children is better than writing books while Simone's position sounds like *The Second Sex* "avant la lettre." She cannot agree on *that*.

Zaza like her friend attends the Sorbonne after they finally manage to convince her conventionally devout father that "you can get a degree without being damned." She wins a certificate in Greek, but she is tormented and unsettled about her future since her family expects her to marry and there always looms the grim prospect of an arranged "suitable" marriage. Romantic in her ideas about marriage, Zaza does not aspire to a career like Simone de Beauvoir, but she is aghast at the spectacle of her sister and other girls being docilely assigned to dull husbands of their parents' choice. Her family are devoutly Catholic and savagely conventional, but Zaza has always loved her mother and is torn by her sense of obedience and her natural desire to be happy; she finds it extremely difficult to rebel against the appalling tyranny of her parents' ambitions for her. Zaza confesses to Simone de Beauvoir in a letter that she is desperately unhappy and recounts to her friend the story of a romantic passion she has had for a cousin from South America which was terminated by the opposition of her parents. She says that she even contemplated suicide. Zaza is extremely romantic in her emotional attachments and, alas, too good. She discovers that literal Christian abnegation can mean despair. She writes: "When I was little, I always used to ask in my prayers: don't ever let anyone suffer because of me. Alas! What an unrealizable prayer!"[6]

Mme. Mabille, a classic dominating mother, becomes alarmed at Zaza's exposure to the wrong people at the Sorbonne and forbids her to continue her studies. She is frankly hostile to Simone de Beauvoir but allows Zaza to invite her to their summer house. Zaza has the courage to defy her mother in a scene which conveys the incredible narrowness and odious "Christian" devotion of Mme. Mabille and shows what poor Zaza is up against. *The Second Sex* is peopled with female gorgons of this type: "One evening however Zaza rebelled. In the middle of dinner Madame Mabille announced in a cutting voice: 'I don't understand how a believer can be friends with an unbeliever.' I felt horribly embarrassed and the blood rushed to my cheeks. Zaza retorted indignantly 'No one has the right to judge anyone else. God leads people in the ways he chooses.' 'I don't judge,' said Madame Mabille coldly, 'We may pray for lost souls, but we will not let ourselves be contaminated by them.' Zaza choked with anger and that restored my serenity."

(MDJFR, p. 267) The only thing one can ever reproach Zaza for is her lack of courage in revolting against her parents, but she has been soundly indoctrinated; otherwise she is always brave and passionately indignant about cruelty and injustice. A long war of attrition is waged between Zaza and her mother and Zaza bravely contends with what can only be called the forces of evil. Madame Mabille has forbidden Zaza to accept an invitation for a tennis game with Simone de Beauvoir and some young friends; this is to mingle (oh horror) with young men whose parents one does not know. Zaza writes of her struggle and she is sardonic about her mother, but respectful: "I wish you could realize this state of mind which I'm up against and which furthermore my Christian ideas oblige me to respect. But today nervous tension from this conflict drives me to tears: the things which I love do not love each other; and under the pretext of moral scruples people have said things I find revolting. I offered ironically to sign a paper by which I would commit myself to never marrying either Pradelle or Clairaut or any of their friends, but that didn't quiet Mama." (MDJFR, p. 276)

Zaza is dispatched to Berlin to escape the evil influences of Paris; she returns and falls in love with Jean Pradelle, a friend of Simone de Beauvoir's. All Madame Mabille's defensive strategy has been in vain. Zaza radiates happiness and is now determined to reject the malignant influence of her family. "Suddenly she had understood with final clarity that she would never again accept the stunting of mind and spirit that her milieu tried to impose upon her." (MDJFR, p. 315) Nevertheless, Zaza suffers the common fate of true goodness in a cruel world. She must continue to battle her mother and Pradelle himself cannot marry her or even announce their engagement because of some absurd consideration for his widowed mother whose other son has just left for South America. Zaza's letter telling of her distress and her feelings for her lover is moving; she is a generous "amoureuse": "Then the thought of his existence is enough to reduce me to tears, and when I reflect that in a small way he exists for me and through me, I feel painfully as if my heart almost stops beating under the weight of too much happiness." However, her goodness in effect kills her; Simone de Beauvoir explains the horrible pressures she is under: "Her grandeur of spirit exasperated me. She understood my wrath; she understood Pardelle's scruples, and Madame Mabille's prudence; she understood all the people who didn't understand each other and whose misunderstandings all redounded on her." (MDJFR, p. 341) Worn out and distraught, Zaza is affected physically by this battle. Simone de Beauvoir sees her off before her second enforced departure for Berlin and she exudes gaiety and hope; she is rereading Stendhal with enthusiasm and talks of writing a novel; but there is something slightly feverish and forced in her optimism. Immediately afterwards she becomes gravely ill; she had appeared at Madame Pradelle's apartment without a hat (sure sign of aberration in this period) and wild-eyed, she had asked Mme. Pradelle why she detested her, why she wouldn't consent to her son's marriage. Pradelle takes her home in a cab and she is put to bed with an alarming fever. The parents rally around her: "Madame Mabille put her to bed and called the doctor; she set things straight with Pradelle; she didn't want her daughter to be unhappy; she wasn't opposed to this marriage. Madame Mabille wasn't going to stand in their way any longer; she didn't want anyone to be unhappy. Everything was going to be all right." (MDJFR, p. 45) But

Zaza dies. Madame Mabille weeps over Zaza at the clinic while M. Mabille comforts her: "We have only been the instruments in the hands of God."

Simone de Beauvoir used the drama of Zaza in her two early abortive attempts at writing a novel, but she never again attempted to create a fictional character based on her friend. Zaza does not seem to belong in Simone de Beauvoir's fictional universe; nor does she belong in *The Second Sex.* She had the kind of qualities that are traditionally regarded as womanly: generosity, gentleness and kindness, but at the same time she was a truly authentic person, strong in her sense of what she was and what she believed. She always gives the impression of strength of character, not docility and meekness because she feels and thinks passionately. It would seem inappropriate to call her a "relative being." Had she lived, she might have written novels or done any number of remarkable things, but one cannot help feeling that she should have been a mother, since she had in such abundance those qualities motherhood demands. Her admirable qualities as a human being were her capacity for love and affection, her lack of egoism and her generosity. It is impossible to think of her in terms of the distinction of *The Second Sex* where a person's human value is measured mainly in terms of his accomplishment and his forceful imprint on the world. It is difficult to see Zaza as a lesser human being than her father or her fiancé, for example.[7] Zaza might fit the category of a person who practices "le dévouement" and in her case it does not seem an impossible or especially ignoble ideal. Sometimes goodness appears to be in even shorter supply in the world than ambition and creative energy, although it certainly does not inspire Simone de Beauvoir. Yet in her moving portrait of Zaza she paints a living incarnation of it. Zaza's special kind of feminine charm and generosity could serve as a faint corrective to the undervaluation of the traditional feminine virtues which is a central premise of *The Second Sex*.

NOTES

1. Geneviève Genarri, *Simone de Beauvoir* (Paris: Editions universitaires, 1959), p. 97.

2. Ibid., p. 98.

3. A pessimist might say with some justice that this is what happens in most cases—if one chooses to view the mass of mankind as miserable creatures, better not to have been born. Yet, Simone de Beauvoir's theory, if assiduously adopted, would only compound the horror. Imagine a hypothetical situation where all women literally shared Simone de Beauvoir's opinions about motherhood. If it were universally thought distasteful and unrewarding, heaven help the children!

4. I refer to *Pyrrhus et Cinéas* not primarily to argue ethical questions, but to show the extent of Simone de Beauvoir's antipathy to "le dévouement." In spite of all the false kinds of generosity, what Simone de Beauvoir calls "le dévouement", one cannot help feeling that if there is no generosity or genuine disinterested love in maternal love, there is none anywhere, since all human affection originates in the mother-child relationship. It is difficult to disagree with the aphorism of Alain: "Maternal love is the model of all love."

5. Georges Hourdin who writes from the Christian point of view points out that in *The Second Sex* Simone de Beauvoir does not admire the celebrated woman mystics and saints for their goodness or spiritual splendor but for their power and worldly success. "What Simone de Beauvoir admires in them is their virility and decisiveness: Saint Theresa of Avila for founding monasteries and Saint Catherine of Siena's political intrigues in the fifteenth-century church to promote the Pope's return to Rome. . . . For Simone de Beauvoir, freedom is not demonstrated until it acquires historical significance through action." Georges Hourdin, *Simone de Beauvoir et la liberté* (Paris: Les Editions du Cerf, 1962), pp. 126–27.

6. Zaza's unhappiness due to her family's oppressive treatment certainly confirms the thesis of *The Second Sex* that the traditional upbringing of young girls is monstrous; her whole history tragically illustrates this. I merely want to show that somehow this did not make her an inferior person; on the contrary, her character reveals "womanly" traits which her upbringing

could not extinguish and may even paradoxically have fostered. Zaza demonstrates that the entire female sex is not necessarily inferior *morally* to the male sex, a basic assumption of *The Second Sex*. There may well be some "feminine" qualities that are worth preserving and encouraging. This in no way denies the claims of militant feminism or contradicts the just demand for equality. Even if women are softer, more gentle, and less aggressive then men (is this bad?), this does not appear to justify assigning them the menial ill-paid jobs and relegating them to the status of a subclass.

7. *The Second Sex* emphatically insists that a person's human worth derives from what he does; it is measured in terms of action, accomplishment, and power. But isn't this almost like saying that a person really *is* his role; a position actually contrary to what existentialism and all the great religions maintain. They hold instead that the true value of a human being resides in his moral qualities. It is self-evident that the powerful and successful of the world are not necessarily the good ones. Work is not irrelevant of course, but the equation of human value and the job one has seems exceedingly simplistic. *The Second Sex* evinces a rather uncritical worship of worldly success.

7

Conclusion

Simone de Beauvoir's preoccupation with the woman question can clearly be seen as one of the dominant motifs of her work. I have shown how her autobiography, her theoretical work on woman's destiny, *The Second Sex,* and the vividly portrayed feminine characters of the novels all reflect her absorption in this timeless but perenially interesting subject.[1] The somber thesis of *The Second Sex* that it is a malediction to be a woman finds substantial support in the novels inasmuch as the feminine characters are preponderantly unhappy, divided and neurotic creatures. Though they do not consciously reflect on their fate and submission *qua* woman, most are nonetheless conspicuously marked by a flaw; one suspects that their suffering derives in part from their initial misfortune of being female. The pessimism of *The Second Sex* is thus reinforced in the novels. However, *The Second Sex* also contains the optimistic and even Utopian idea that woman's subjection and role as the passive, "inessential" being has arbitrarily been imposed by the dominant male culture. If woman could become economically independent and as committed to her work as man she might escape the curse of immanence, passivity, and relative "being." "One is not born a woman, one becomes one" expresses Simone de Beauvoir's radical conception that the unhappiness of woman is rooted in culture and not biology. Woman is thus in principle capable of transcending her inferiority, which is man-made. *The Second Sex* appears in that perspective as an exhortation to women to rise from their passivity and indifference and break the chains which enslave them.

The "ideal" of *The Second Sex* is this future emancipated woman, but the vast documentation of the book produces a very negative and uninspiring picture of woman as she has been and actually is. Woman has been sadly impaired by her role as wife, mother, amoureuse, etc. As a result, and ideal theory notwithstanding, by and large the pessimistic element of woman's malediction and inferiority to man dominates the work. This "objective" description does not have to obtain for fictional works. It is there that the ideal woman could be found. Indeed, I have shown that two of Simone de Beauvoir's fictional heroines, Françoise in *L'Invitée* and Anne in *Les Mandarins,* both modeled on Simone de Beauvoir herself, represent in some measure the emancipated woman. They both have careers that make them economically independent of men and they are also "sympathetic" heroines. They have generosity of spirit, intelligence, some strength, and a grandeur of character that quite sets them apart from the mournful array of *The Second Sex* females whose pettiness, self-pity, passivity, resentment and subtle domination through feminine martyrdom produce such an unsavory impression of women in general. They are also infinitely more prepossessing as human beings than the other "sad" feminine characters of the novels. And yet neither Anne nor Françoise is really an "emancipated" woman, for both suffer from some inexplicable weakness which makes them unable to assert themselves with the full vigor of an authentic, liberated personality. Françoise has an almost pathological de-

pendence on Pierre, while Anne not only is an "amoureuse" whose life is almost ruined by the unhappy end
of a love affair, but she succumbs to despair in middle age
and contemplates suicide. Both Anne and Françoise for
some mysterious reason regard their work as subsidiary
and relegate it to a minor role even though it must consume large quantities of time and energy conveniently
ignored by the conventions of novel writing.

Possibly the key to Simone de Beauvoir's ambiguous
feelings can be discerned in Françoise and Anne, who
express her own emotional difficulties. Like Françoise
with Pierre, Simone de Beauvoir was exceedingly dependent on the opinions of Sartre; the autobiography continually documents this: "There was no question of disa-
greeing with him about it since I could not bear any
discord between him and me." (LFDL'A, p. 294) Similarly, Anne's love affair (though treated with sympathy
and approval she is "une amoureuse" who lets her love
life dominate her life) is autobiographical, and her despair in face of the onslaught of desolate middle age is
exactly recapitulated in *La Force des Choses* with its chilling
finale of "la femme flouée"—an avowal that significantly
undermines the entire hopeful thesis of *The Second Sex.*

The dramas of Françoise and Anne are the drama of
Simone de Beauvoir. And though *one* example of ideal
emancipated woman, namely herself, is postulated in the
autobiography—Simone de Beauvoir insists that she herself has escaped the malediction in following her own
precepts—one must conclude that her identification of
emancipation with serene independence and strength is
perhaps not altogether valid. Simone de Beauvoir suffered from the same weaknesses as her heroines; in the
novels these weaknesses are not seen as necessarily reprehensible where they emerge as part of the imponderable

complexity of the anguished human condition. Yet according to the implacable standards of *The Second Sex* they must be seen as failings which prevent either heroine from achieving that tranquil state of strength and wisdom so wistfully extolled in *The Second Sex*—that is, the same authenticity and freedom as the male enjoys. Thus Anne and Françoise are in a sense self-criticism on the part of the author. They may serve as an ironic rejoinder to Simone de Beauvoir's assertion that she herself has indeed escaped the malediction of womankind by adhering to her precepts of creative work and economic independence and by having renounced the debilitating roles of wife and mother. Furthermore, Simone de Beauvoir's treatment of Françoise and Anne can perhaps help to account for the violence of Simone de Beauvoir's attack on the traditional "feminine" virtues. Simone de Beauvoir not only scorns female passivity and dependence but somehow links traditional feminine qualities like gentleness, kindness, unselfish devotion etc. to weakness. Her entire attack on "le dévouement" seems to stem from an aversion to the conventional "maternal" quality in woman so "hypocritically" praised by men through the ages. While her favored catalogue of virtues always contains the traditional masculine traits of power, domination, action, etc., she often talks as though goodness or gentleness were positive defects. Surely this is a strange overestimation of power and strength at the expense of other indispensable human qualities. Anne for instance worries about being "too attached" to her family. Yet it is not really her attachment to her family that seems misguided but some inner weakness and lack of self-assertion. One gets the impression that Simone de Beauvoir's horror of dependence and passivity in women arises both from the undeniable subjugation of women as a class, but also from some weakness or dependency in herself which she deplores. Therefore, she identifies "dependence" and "weakness" with all the classic feminine virtues, excoriates "le dévouement" as a perversion of familial affection, and even casts grave doubts on familial affection itself. Psychological "dependency" is a very complex phenomenon, often not recognized by the victim. The equation of economic independence and inner psychic freedom seems somewhat simplistic, but is perhaps understandable in the light of Simone de Beauvoir's own tendencies. Anne and Françoise both show that economic independence is not enough; Simone de Beauvoir's "ideal" woman remains an ideal.

As for woman as she is, or was yesterday, Simone de Beauvoir frankly confesses that she describes women as she sees them—as "divided beings." Thus Paule, Hélène, Denise, Elisabeth, Régine, Nadine and Xavière and the legion of discontented females of *The Second Sex* represent the *choice* of Simone de Beauvoir; they are finely etched portraits of various types of femininity and they personify in a compelling way the pessimistic and anti-feminine bias of *The Second Sex:* woman has not only been cruelly oppressed by man, but the limitations on her freedom and the imposition of a specifically feminine role have hindered her from exemplifying humanity at its best. Woman remains inferior, unable to surmount the tragic handicaps of her cultural situation. The heroines of the novels, products of Simone de Beauvoir's imagination, illustrate in a more complex and interesting way the tragic theme of *The Second Sex.* They represent the depth and consistency of her deepest convictions on the subject.

Simone de Beauvoir's theory itself which is, in my opinion, unjust to women, is presented in an extreme and somewhat simplistic manner as I have often indicated. Such a rigorously one-sided polemic has difficulty in maintaining itself and there are moments when the weaknesses show through. At such moments Simone de Beauvoir comes precariously close to admitting the insufficiency of her one-sided doctrine. *The Second Sex* staunchly insists that transcendence, action, creativity, and power are the masculine virtues par excellence, and these are what determine human value. Being, passivity, and immanence are feminine prerogatives and they diminish the human value of those trapped in this mode of existence. Action and transcendence are male and good; being and immanence are feminine and bad. Unless women renounce "femininity" and equal men on their own terms, they will continue to be inferior. Essentially, therefore, Simone de Beauvoir seems to equate a person's human value and moral worth with his role: the kind of work one does determines human excellence. This does seem a bit questionable and at odds with a more philosophical analysis of human worth. If Simone de Beauvoir merely meant to describe what the world values and respects, she would have been justified. The world always worships power and success and the tangible evidence of it. And the world does indeed regard women as inferior, which is why they are up in arms today. But to literally equate human worth with power and success does not seem to be very profound. At any rate the undisguised adulation of "masculine" activity becomes not only fatiguing but arouses a certain skepticism; the tone is always extravagant and romantic as though all masculine "action" were the equivalent of adventure and creative genius and not simply going down to the office and earning a living. Does this lyrical rhapsody of masculine activity really ring true? At last

Simone de Beauvoir herself, more *terre-à-terre,* imagines what these adventurers and heroes will be doing; for a moment reality intrudes and the theory is in danger of collapse. After concluding that woman's situation and her role have been responsible for her inferiority as a human being, Simone de Beauvoir reflects on the facts, and the result is quite unexpected: . . . . "The fact that transcendence is denied her keeps her as a rule from the loftiest human attitudes: heroism, revolt, disinterestedness, imagination, creation; but even among the males they are none too common." (TSS, II, p. 588) From here Simone de Beauvoir envisages the common run of masculine endeavor, man's "transcendence: as it were, in the factory and at the office; throwing her previous arguments to the winds, she becomes eloquent about the moral inferiority of the male. The horrors of conformism, dullness, unimaginative pomposity, and ignoble money-grubbing are seen to be his lot and his situation in turn damages his character almost beyond repair. Everything is reversed and freedom, authenticity, imagination and moral superiority are actually deemed to be encouraged by the freer and more enviable life of "the housewife!" It is a breath-taking switch and Simone de Beauvoir's euphoric description of the positive aspects of woman's traditional role is delightful hyperbole, but decidedly un-Beauvoirian! It is the mere thought of the mediocre run-of-the-mill average specimen of mankind, especially in his middle-class manifestation, that elicits this rare panegyric to woman and the untold benefits of her traditional role. Here is the unbearable stuffy bureaucrat versus his superior and delightful wife:

> Destined like woman to the repetition of daily tasks, identified with ready-made values, respectful of public opinion, and seek-

ing naught on earth but a vague comfort, the employee, the merchant, the office worker, are in no way superior to their accompanying females. Cooking, washing, managing her house, bringing up children, woman shows more initiative and independence than the man slaving under orders. All day long he must obey his superiors, wear a white collar, and keep up his social standing; she can dawdle around the apartment in a wrapper, sing, laugh with her neighbors; she does as she pleases, takes little risks, tries to succeed in getting certain results. She lives less than her husband in an atmosphere of conventional concern for appearances.

This office universe . . . . this universe of formalities, of absurd gestures, of purposeless behavior, is essentially masculine. Woman gets her teeth more deeply into reality; for when the office worker has drawn up his figures, or translated boxes of sardines into money, he has nothing in his hands but abstractions. The baby fed and in his cradle, clean linen, the roast, constitute more tangible assets; yet just because, in the concrete pursuit of these aims, she feels their contingence—and accordingly her own—it often happens that woman does not identify herself with them, and she still has something left of herself. Man's enterprises are at once projects and evasions: he lets himself be smothered by his career and his "front"; he often becomes self-important, weighty. Being against man's logic and morality, woman does not fall into these traps, which Stendhal found much to his taste in her; she does not take refuge in her pride from the ambiguity of her position; she does not hide behind the mask of human dignity; she reveals her undisciplined thoughts, her emotions, her spontaneous reactions more frankly. Thus her conversation is much less tiresome than her husband's whenever she speaks for herself and not as her lord and master's loyal "better half." [TSS, II, pp. 588–89]

This is an engaging exaggeration, but it demonstrates the weakness of Simone de Beauvoir's all-or-nothing approach. At any rate, the two rather absurd extremes might indicate that perhaps there is something not entirely sound in measuring the human quality or merit of individuals by virtue of their role or function. The whole point of feminism is based on the idea of justice and equality, and judgments about the relative merits of masculine or feminine virtues seem to be a bit irrelevant. This aspect of Simone de Beauvoir's thesis is often irritating because it is unjust and beside the point. Women want equal treatment and justice, and do not need lectures on the superiority of masculine virtues and how they should strive to attain them.

The most brilliant section of *The Second Sex* is Simone de Beauvoir's analysis of several myths about woman propagated by various male writers. Her sympathetic and astute discussion of Stendhal, who was a feminist, champion, and idolater of women, provides a very penetrating counterargument to her own general denigration of them. Stendhal held that it is paradoxically the oppression of women that enables them (the best of them) to escape the worst faults of their oppressors. Excluded from power, they are able to look with skepticism and irony on all the values the world holds so dear. Like artists, intellectuals or slaves or any group effectively denied power they can judge the true values from the false and be moral critics because they are barred from participation in the always compromised moral paltriness of actual power. Stendhal loathed "le monde sérieux" and his most winning heroines always demonstrate a luminous capacity to unveil the *idées reçues* and absurd pretentions of this world. (TSS, I, pp. 225–26) Thus Stendhal's heroines embody the qualities he admires most—their role or place in the world of affairs does not coincide with or determine their human worth—*au contraire*. These marvelous heroines finally triumph over their subservient condition because they know what the true values are: they are "dans les coeurs." Weak and dependent as they are, they are morally superior beings. Simone de Beauvoir describes them with zest and admiration. Here she shares Stendhal's enthusiasm and seems to concur with him that it is not action and power as much as the moral qualities of character and sensibility that determine human excellence. The true values are "dans les coeurs." She describes Stendhal's women:

> These women are, quite simply, *alive;* they know that the source of true values is not in external things but in human hearts. This gives its charm to the world they live in: they banish ennui by the simple fact of their presence, with their dreams, their desires, their pleasures, their emotions, their ingenuities. The Sanserverina, that "active soul," dreads ennui more than death. To stagnate in ennui "is to keep from dying, she said, not to live"; she is "always impassioned over something, always in action, and gay, too." Thoughtless, childish or profound; gay or grave, daring or secretive, they all reject the heavy sleep in which humanity is mired. And these women who have been able to maintain their liberty—empty as it has been—will rise through passion to heroism once they find an objective worthy of them; their spiritual power, their energy, suggest the fierce purity of total dedication. [TSS, I, pp. 226–27]

Simone de Beauvoir's own heroines are certainly made in a different and less exhilarating mold, because they reflect her own disenchantment with woman's lot and a gloomier philosophy. Nonetheless in this acute analysis of Stendhal's "myth" about woman Simone de Beauvoir demonstrates the infinite and tantalizing complexity of the problem, which can never be adequately disposed of in reductive theories such as her own. She finally praises Stendhal because in spite of his romanticism and exaltation of woman she maintains that he actually refuses the myths and embraces the much more satisfying human

reality. Here the romantic and realist Simone de Beauvoir joins the romantic but realist Stendhal, and this attitude toward the second sex is perhaps the most appealing
of all. For Stendhal the charm and excellence of woman
comes from her status (in his eyes) as a free and equal
human being and not as a creature of fantasy invented by
man to nourish his own grandiose and unreal dreams
about himself as a being whose worth is measured by
power and domination. As Simone de Beauvoir says
about Stendhal: "That is why he rejects the mystifications
of the serious, as he rejects the false poetry of the myths.
Human reality suffices him. Woman according to him is
simply a human being: nor could any shape of dreams be
more enrapturing." (TSS, I, p. 233)

NOTES

1. It is at any rate interesting to a small part of one half of the human race.
The boredom and indifference of men to the "woman question," especially
as it touches on the implacable exclusion of women from power and equal
opportunity, perhaps merits sociological and psychological exploration.

Postscript

SIMONE DE BEAUVOIR AND WOMEN'S LIBERATION

Today the worldwide movement for women's liberation proves the relevance of Simone de Beauvoir's brand
of feminism. After centuries of unjust domination
women are at last becoming aware of the necessity for
real equality. The message of *The Second Sex* that women
are an oppressed class has finally begun to penetrate the
consciousness of women everywhere who realize how
their total conditioning through male-dominated institutions has blinded them to the truth of their very real
unequal and inferior place in human society. Simone de
Beauvoir's work has become a classic in feminist literature and she deserves to be honored for her very great
contribution to women's liberation. If I have been critical
of a part of her theory, I must still render her homage for
her original, penetrating and sympathetic advancement
of the cause. Her analysis of the subtle and insinuating
way women are molded by society to accept their inferior
role is masterful and devastating. Her perception of how
the male-dominated culture tries to transform woman
into an "object" who exists primarily to please men has
had profound reverberations and has been taken over by
the Women's Liberation movement as part of its elo-

219

quent indictment of the inhumanity of man to woman. Above all, her attempt to delineate how woman's oppression does not depend so much on legal exclusion (they can vote, can't they?) as on massive social conditioning of male and female so that "sexism" dominates all of our judgments, represents a pioneer advance in the feminist movement. Her exposure of the total and absolute manner in which role-conditioning and centuries of male-dominated history and culture have enveloped woman in a miasma of misconceptions about herself and insured her passivity and powerlessness is brilliant. *The Second Sex,* whose insights are common coin in feminist arguments today, is an astonishing revelation of how successful social conditioning can be: no slave class has ever been so thoroughly indoctrinated to accept and even enjoy its oppression as the second sex. Woman's subjugation is a stunning and unparalleled example of social blackmail on a grand scale and *The Second Sex* was the first publication to unmask this in a concentrated polemical attack. Yes, Simone de Beauvoir is a heroine in women's liberation and will certainly be accorded an honorable place in the history of that movement.

Women's liberation, however, would not accord as much respect to "masculine" virtues as does Simone de Beauvoir. In fact, the adulation of "masculine" virtues and depreciation of "feminine" ones by some feminists seems to prove the very point feminists make about the pervasiveness of the values which a male-dominated society imposes. The current feminist movement exalts femininity and the gentle, maternal, sensitive traits that are encouraged in women. It holds, sensibly, that these qualities should be encouraged in everyone. It emphasizes these qualities, not only because they are intrinsically valuable (indeed necessary for survival), but also to help restore to women their self-respect and dignity. Women's liberationists are justly outraged by the way society destroys woman's confidence in herself and her sense of her own worth, by excluding her from equal participation in society, confining her to one role, and therefore producing to everyone's satisfaction the evidence that she is inferior. Their movement is not narrowly legalistic, but a profound critique of Western civilization which gives lip service to charity, compassion, and goodness but whose real gods are domination, aggressiveness, competitiveness, and power. As Ashley Montagu remarks, the real values of a society that children intuit are to be discovered not in what people say but in what they do, and in our society all the prizes go to competitiveness, aggression, and even ruthlessness which is not really scorned but secretly admired. Women's Liberation is attacking the moral schizophrenia at the heart of our culture.

In many ways women are superior to men and it is time that they recognize this. The very fact that they are brought up as they are insures their having in a larger degree those traits which we praise and know to be good, but depreciate in actuality since the masculine world demands aggressiveness and cut-throat competitiveness and regards sensitivity and idealism with a jaundiced eye: it is not "pragmatic," or "realist" or "efficient" to worry about the human side of a question. That is to be too "feminine", too "emotional." Simone de Beauvoir's misogyny disturbs me because twenty centuries of misogareyny is enough. Women are not inferior human beings, they are oppressed, and it is time they proudly hold up their heads and proclaim their own worth. Feminist critics should not add fuel to the ancient irrational and unjust claims of male chauvinists about woman's inferiority.

The depths of male prejudice only begin to surface when women seek genuine equality. The scorn, outrage, spite and sheer terror that women's liberation produces in even "liberal" male critics is a frightening indication of the tenacity and power of the prejudice that centuries of male-domination have instilled in people's minds. Why women even have to argue for their right to equal treatment is beyond me, but they do.

Alexis de Tocqueville, a brilliant, cultivated and enlightened Frenchman who was in fact a particular admirer of American womanhood, wrote the following about democracy in America." "In the United States, except slaves, servants and paupers supported by the townships, there is no class of persons who do not exercise the elective franchise and who do not indirectly contribute to make the laws. Those who wish to attack the laws must consequently either change the opinion of the nation or trample upon its decision."[1] De Tocqueville cannot be blamed for his moral opacity in omitting one half of the population of the United States in his analysis. Women simply did not exist as persons and citizens in his mind. Men have always found it convenient and easy to think of women as non-persons and the vestiges of this attitude are still incredibly strong. So, in order to "change the opinion of the nation" women must unite in sisterhood and demonstrate what we've always really known that they are equal, not inferior, human beings, and that what the world needs desperately is not less but more femininity *in action,* because civilization is always in danger of relapsing into barbarism. Ashley Montagu says it well: "Civilization is the art of being kind, an art that women have learned much better than men."[2]

NOTES

1. Alexis de Tocqueville, *Democracy in America,* ed. Phillips Bradley (New York: Vintage Press, 1955), 1: 257.

2. Ashley Montagu, *The Natural Superiority of Women* (New York: Collier Books, 1970), p. 204.

Selected Bibliography

Beauvoir, Simone de. *L'Invitée.* Paris: Gallimard, 1943.
_____. *Le Sang des Autres.* Paris: Gallimard, 1945.
_____. *Tous les Hommes Sont Mortels.* Paris: Gallimard, 1946.
_____. *Les Mandarins.* Paris: Gallimard, 1954.
_____. *Le Deuxième Sexe I: Les Faits et Les Mythes.* Paris: Gallimard, 1949.
_____. *Le Deuxième Sexe II: L'Expérience Vécue.* Paris: Gallimard, 1949.
_____. *The Second Sex.* Translated and edited by H. M. Parshley. New York: Alfred A. Knopf, Inc., 1962. (Bantam edition, 1961)
_____. *Pour une morale de l'ambiguité* suivie de *Pyrrhus et Cinéas.* Paris: Gallimard, 1966.
_____. *Memoires d'une Jeune Fille Rangée.* Paris: Gallimard, 1958.
_____. *La Force de L'Age.* Paris: Gallimard, 1960.
_____. *La Force des Choses.* Paris: Gallimard, 1963.
Barnes, Hazel E. *Humanistic Existentialism: The Literature of Possibility.* Lincoln, Nebraska: University of Nebraska Press, 1959.
Gennari, Geneviève. *Simone de Beauvoir.* Paris: Editions universitaires, 1959.
Hourdin, Georges. *Simone de Beauvoir et la Liberté.* Paris: Les Editions du Cerf, 1962.
Montagu, Ashley. *The Natural Superiority of Women.* New York: Collier Books, 1970.

Tocqueville, Alexis de. *Democracy in America.* 2 vols. Edited by Phillips Bradley. New York: Vintage Books, 1955.

Articles and Periodicals

Algren, Nelson. "The Question of Simone de Beauvoir." *Harper's* (May 1965), pp. 134–36.

Aury, Dominique. "Personne ne triche." *La Nouvelle Nouvelle Revue Française,* 2e année, no. 24 (Dec.1954), pp. 1080–85.

Blin, Georges. "Simone de Beauvoir et le problème de l'action." *Fontaine,* no. 45 (1 Oct.1945), pp. 716–30.

Bousquet, Joé. "Simone de Beauvoir et la poésie." *Critique,* no. 12 (May 1947), pp. 390–93.

Hardwick, Elizabeth. "The Subjection of Women." *Partisan Review* 20, no. 3 (May–June 1953): 321–31.

Hentoff, Margot. "The Curse." *New York Review of Books* (Jan. 16, 1969), p. 3.

Merleau-Ponty, Maurice. "Le roman et la métaphysique," *Sens et Non-Sens,* edited by Nagel. Paris, 1948, 12: 51–81.

Weightman, J. G. "Growing up in Paris." *Encounter* 13, no. 2 (August, 1959): 77–81.

Index

Abelard, 114
Adolescence, feminine. *See* Girls
Algren, Nelson, 102, 114
Altruism, 169, 191, 193–94
Anne (character in *Les Mandarins*), 74, 76–113; as "amoureuse, 76, 96–105, 108; as autobiographical portrait of Simone de Beauvoir, 82–93, 107, 110–13, 131, 209–12; existentialist proclivities of, 87–93, 104–6, 108–10; as mother, 96, 171–75, 180–81; old age complex of, 92–94, 105–6, 108
l'Amoureuse, 72–73, 78–81, 96–102, 122, 126, 128, 204
Aristotle, 39
Aury, Dominique, 97, 113–14, 159, 170
Austen, Jane, 145

Balzac, 39, 79
Barnes, Hazel, 51
Bashkirtsev, Marie, 131–32
Beauvoir, Simone de: anti-feminine bias of, 39–40, 45, 70–71, 93, 95, 107, 115–19, 129–30, 146–48, 209–12; character and temperament of, 29–30, 73, 75, 83–84, 88–93, 110–13, 116, 127–28, 176, 194–97; childhood of, 26–27, 153–56, 194–97; extremism of, 26–27, 45–46, 86, 110, 176; father of, 44, 156–59; fear of dependence in, 73, 75, 83–84, 93,

210–12; "femininity" of, 41–43, 154–59; feminism of, 17, 21, 115, 188, 209; on *L'Invitée*, 52; as model of ideal emancipated woman, 20, 41, 53, 210–12; mother of, 44, 156, 197–98; on old age, 91–93, 110–13; optimism of, 38; pessimism of, 38, 110–12, 183, 188, 208; and Sartre, 55–60, 65–66, 79–90, 114, 210; on *The Second Sex*, 17, 41, and Women's Liberation, 219–21
Blin, Georges, 51, 74–75
Blomart, Jean (character in *Le Sang des Autres*), 126, 128–30
Blue Beard, 141
Bousquet, Joé, 138
Brogan, Lewis. *See* Lewis
Brontë, Emily, 143
Brontës, the, 145

Caesar Borgia, 141
Camille, 140–47
Childbirth, 32, 185–86
Christie, Agatha, 53
Claude (character in *L'Invitée*), 133–35

Denise (character in *Le Sang des Autres*), 136–37
"Le Dévouement," 191–94, 198, 211
Dodge, Mabel, 123
Drouet, Juliette, 77

227

Dubreuilh, Anne. *See* Anne Dubreuilh, Robert (character in *Les Mandarins*), 85–87
Dullin, Charles, 142, 146
Dürer, Albrecht, 143

Eliot, George, 145, 151
Elisabeth (character in *L'Invitée*), 132–35
L'Etre et le Néant, 51, 69, 75
Existentialism. *See* Existentialist philosophy
Existentialist philosophy, 31–33, 52, 88–94, 118, 167, 169, 185–86

Family life, 190, 192, 196
Feminine psychology, 34, 80, 95, 113; importance of love in, 72–73, 78–79
Feminine virtues, 21, 194, 198, 205–6, 211, 214–16, 220–21
Femininity, 36, 41–43, 151, 173, 178, 182–83, 222
Feminism, 3–31, 115, 185, 188, 216
Françoise (character in *L'Invitée*), 48–75, 135, 162–69; as autobiographical portrait of Simone de Beauvoir, 49, 107, 131, 209–11
Freud, Sigmund, 40–41
Fosca (character in *Le Sang des Autres*), 138–40

Girls, 35, 150–183; good qualities of, 153, 155, 165

Hegel, 46, 51
Hélène (character in *Le Sang des Autres*), 125–31
Héloise, 108, 114
Henri (character in *Les Mandarins*), 84, 119–24, 174–78

Housewife, 214–15
Housework, 90, 196
Hugo, Victor, 77

Jealousy, 59–60, 63–65, 69

Kosakievicz, Olga, 50, 159–62

Labrousse, Pierre. *See* Pierre
La Force de l'Age, 18, 41–42, 48–50, 53, 57–58, 60, 65–66, 82, 116, 130, 141–44, 146, 159–62, 210
La Force des Choses, 17–20, 25, 83–84, 91, 102, 106–7, 110–12, 125, 136, 140, 170, 210
Lambert (character in *Les Mandarins*), 179–81
Lawrence, D. H., 123
Lawrence, T. E., 181
Leblanc, Georgette, 123
Leiris, Michel, 25
Lenin, 46
Le Sang des Autres, 25, 125–31, 136–37
Les Mandarins, 27, 74, 76–113, 119–25, 169–83, 209
Lévi-Strauss, Claude, 154
Lewis (character in *Les Mandarins*), 92, 94, 97–103, 105
L'Invitée, 25, 48–74, 132–35, 159–69, 209
Little Women (Alcott), 151
Louis XI, 141
Love: authentic, 79, 98–102, "necessary" and "contingent," 57, 114; overestimation of in women, 72–73, 78–79, 98, 127
Lucifer, 141
Luther, Martin, 39

Mabille, Elisabeth. *See* Zaza
Maeterlinck, Maurice, 123
Mailer, Norman, 187

Male, the: overestimation of, 44–45, 78–80, 179, 211; superiority of, 30, 32–33, 44–45, 80, 152
Male prejudice, 151, 222
Marcel (character in *Le Sang des Autres*), 136–37
Masculine virtues, 21, 32–34, 39, 193–94, 211, 213, 220–21
Maternity. *See* motherhood
Mauriac, Claude, 46
Mémoires d'une Jeune Fille Rangée, 18, 26–27, 29–30, 41, 43–44, 56, 85, 90, 128, 153–58, 194–205
Merleau-Ponty, Maurice, 51, 74, 154
Michelet, 39–40, 141
Miguel, Françoise. *See* Françoise
Misogyny, 39, 115–19, 129–30, 147, 212, 221
Montagu, Ashley, 221–22
Motherhood, 24, 28–29, 185–206

Nadine (character in *Les Mandarins*), 84, 96, 113, 121, 169–83
Narcissism, feminine, 28, 94, 123–25, 128, 131–32, 137–48
Nietzsche, Friedrich, 46, 79, 141, 143

Oblanoff, Lise, 17–172

Pagès, Xavière. *See* Xavière
Paul, Saint, 39, 46
Paule (character in *Les Mandarins*), 84, 103, 119–25
Perron, Henri. *See* Henri
Peter the Cruel, 141
Pierre (character in *L'Invitée*), 50, 52–55, 58–59, 62–63, 66–70, 72, 75, 132, 135, 164, 166–69
Poupette, 156
Psychology, male, 30
Pyrrhus et Cinéas, 25, 192–93

Régine (character in *Tous les Hommes Sont Mortels*), 137–40

Sartre, Jean-Paul, 25, 42, 48, 51, 82, 141–43; and Simone de Beauvoir, 55–58, 60, 65–66, 79–80, 111, 114, 210
Second Sex, The, 17–18, 20, 26–47, 53–55, 63, 70–83, 90–94, 98–100, 102–3, 107–8, 112–13, 115–19, 121, 123, 125, 127, 129, 132–35, 137, 139–40, 145–48, 150–51, 153–58, 165–67, 172, 176–79, 181–83, 185–91, 193, 197, 205–6, 208–19, 220
Sexism, 220
Sincerity: difficulty of, 73; between men and women, 66
Stendhal, 40; women characters of, 216–18

Tocqueville, Alexis de, 222
Tous les Hommes Sont Mortels, 137–40

Values: feminine, 21, 194, 198, 205–6, 211, 214–16, 220–21; masculine, 21, 32–34, 39, 193–94, 211, 213, 220–21
Vigée-Lebrun, Mme., 132

War, glorification of by male culture, 33
Weightman, J. G., 75
Woman: animality of, 117–18; bad characters of, 70–71, 113, 115–20, 123, 125, 129–31, 135, 146–48, 155, 181, 208–10; bad fate of, 17, 42, 45, 115–20, 125, 137, 152–53, 169, 183, 209; biological predicament of, 34, 46, 152, 185–87; dependence of, 42–45, 73, 75, 77, 82–84, 113; the insincere sex, 118, 132, 153; as "ob-

ject," 113, 133, 150, 153, 219; passivity of, 46, 70, 73, 150, 186–88; situation of, 34, 55, 70, 72, 125

Women: martyrdom of, 191, 196, 209; old age in, 91–94, 108

Women artists, 131–49

Women writers, 144–45

Women's Liberation, 33, 219–22

Woolf, Virginia, 145

Xavière (character in *L'Invitée*), 49–50, 53, 59, 62, 67–70, 72, 74, 113, 135, 159–69

Zaza, 199–206